This Too Shall Pass

A Story of Enterprise Banking Company
And Its CEO

By: Hans M. Broder, Jr.

DEDICATION

This Book is dedicated to those who invested their money, devoted their time and energy, and supported the Bank through their patronage; Jim Dorsey and in memory of Glenn Dorsey, who made the partnership possible, and the people of Abbeville who lost their community bank.

ACKNOWLEDGMENTS

I extend my deepest apologies to those who suffered financially or personally by their association with Enterprise. It is my desire that all those that have been impacted by the Bank be aware of the events that took place and understand what transpired.

I am empathetic to the shareholders, including my Broder siblings, who invested in the venture with great expectations but were rewarded with disappointments. I value the support by the members of the Boards at McDonough and Abbeville during the difficult times. But most of all I owe a great deal of thanks to the Officers and Staff that worked tirelessly to make Enterprise Banking Company a proud institution and then only to see it taken away.

My thanks to my daughter, Mia, who organized and prepared my text for print. My appreciation goes to my daughter, Ashlee, and my wife, Lyndy and others, who reviewed the text and corrected most of my typos, misspellings, and bad grammar. I am also very appreciative to others who gave me guidance and motivation to publish this book.

TABLE OF CONTENTS

PREFACE

I was the CEO and had dedicated my banking career to two community banks. The last was Enterprise Banking Company to which I will respectfully refer to as "Enterprise". Enterprise had its roots in Abbeville, Georgia, but the story will center on Henry County, the relocated headquarters of Enterprise and my home.

The following narrative details the creation, evolution, and final days of Enterprise Banking Company and its parent company, Enterprise Banking Company, Inc. Although the plight of the Bank is well known, I will explain the circumstances that led up to the disappointing outcome. Much of what I am about to tell comes from my experience, newspaper articles, and what few records I kept. I admit that I am somewhat biased in how I interpreted the events. Some of my views are critical of others but are intended to be taken in a constructive way. I hope to offer some insight as to the factors and the events that led to the Bank's demise. I will also provide some alternatives that could have minimized the damage to the community banks.

I may bore you with my discussion of the operations and inter-workings of community banks and Enterprise. Since loans were an intricate part of a bank's balance sheet, much will be mentioned about the lending process. I will discuss the roles of the various agencies that regulated Enterprise along with their many regulations they enforced. And finally, there is discussion about the law makers, whose legislative actions impacted Enterprise. Enterprise's Board and Officers faced many challenges while attempting to steer the Bank through a sea of difficulties that made survival an impossibility.

I will share with you my background, my banking experiences, and my personal tribulations. I will discuss the legal problems that arose, and how they were finally resolved. All are portions of my personal banking odyssey that began in 1971 and ended 35 years later in 2016.

CHAPTER ONE

ENTERPRISE: THE BEGINNING

In 2004 Gerald Hudgins approached me and asked if I would be interested in starting a new bank. At first, I did not have any particular desire in managing another bank. I was in retirement just four years removed from The First State Bank (which I will refer to as First State). Financially, I was doing well. My rental property, Rum Creek Golf, and my development ventures were profitable. Since Lyndy and I had accumulated a large number of Henry County Bancshares, Inc. stock (First State), we were receiving regular quarterly dividends. I left First State with a severance package that included some deferred compensation and a comfortable 401k which I had accumulated over my 30 years at the bank. I saw no reason to get back into banking. I had been offered bank management positions and board seats which I had already declined.

When I left First State, I had achieved all of my career goals as a banker. First State had surpassed $400 million in total assets and had at one time 40% of the bank deposit market share in Henry County. First State was considered one of the most successful community banks in the state. The bank had come a long way from the small $10 million bank that I was asked to manage in 1975. To my good fortune, I inherited a great staff and many loyal customers. My role as CEO could not have come at a better time as north Henry County began to experience rapid residential and commercial growth. First State became the primary lender in the area and served as a catalyst to the community's development. First State became a very profitable bank and was able to reward its shareholders.

The accomplishments of First State were a great source of pride for me. I also enjoyed my involvement in the various civil organizations I was asked to participate. I seldom turned down such requests as I felt that banking and community leadership went hand and hand. I had the privilege of serving as Board Chairman of the Henry County Chamber Commerce. At one time or another, I was a member of numerous organizations from Boy Scouts, United Way, Red Cross, Henry Arts Alliance, SPLOST, and Council of Quality Growth to name a few. I also served on the Henry Hospital Medical Operating Board. I am proud that my committee recommended its merger with Piedmont Hospital. My civic involvement earned me a Roast by the Friends of Henry County Library, a memorable event.

The influence of statewide banking brought increased competition and subsequently reduced First State's market share. The Board, which had always supported my management style, now wanted to adopt an aggressive "sales culture" philosophy. It felt that the role for the lenders, including the CEO, was business development. One was expected to make sales calls to pursue deposits and loans for the bank. The primary focus was to target builders and developers. I was a "relationship banker". I never felt comfortable trying to buy someone's banking business. In most cases these potential borrowers required loan pricing concessions and more liberal lending terms. The majority of these borrowers would have no long-term loyalties to the bank. The "sales culture" concept, nevertheless, was the coming trend in the banking industry and became a necessary strategy to remain competitive.

First State had now amassed a very talented and competent management staff. I had accumulated many outside interests that were conflicting with my demanding duties as CEO. I knew that it was probably time to leave after 30 years. There were several challenging business opportunities awaiting me outside of the banking world.

In 2004 the local economy was striving, and the future, likewise, appeared very rosy. The banking business was booming... a trend that began with the advent of the 1996 Olympics and lasted unabated for the next sixteen years. Several Olympic events were held on the southside of Atlanta that summer with "Beach Volley-ballers" competing within an earshot of Henry County. It was an exciting time as the metro area was being showcased on the world stage.

The 1990s witnessed Henry County becoming the sixth fastest growing county, statistically, in the United States. The number of new homes constructed in the Atlanta area and on the southside was unprecedented. Residential construction in 2004 would not peak for another year and continued into the new millennium. The year 2005 saw 2,939 new housing starts. The population of Henry County grew to 200,000 during this period...a far cry from the 24,928 residents when I began my banking career.

The banks never had it better. The publicly traded banks were among the most reliable and consistent dividend payers. Community banks were sought after by larger banks who were willing to pay two to three times the community bank's actual book value. Bank shareholders were being rewarded with regular dividends and continuous appreciation in their stock. In light of the recent investment performance by banks, ownership in another bank appeared to be a wise decision.

After further deliberation, I now considered the organization of a new bank as an interesting undertaking. I knew that I could not immediately duplicate the success of First State, but the long-term benefits appeared too promising to pass up. Even with the increased number of banks doing business in Henry County, the opportunity of leaving a legacy to my family was intriguing. I accepted the challenge and agreed to devote my energies in the pursuit of a new bank. Once the bank was opened and operational, I would step aside as President. A new CEO would be hired to manage the day-to-day affairs of the bank. My role would then shift to serving as a part-time in-house Chairman.

I emphasized the importance to Gerald of having controlling interest in the bank. I knew I could count on his support in allowing me the freedom to organize all the areas of the bank. Like Frank Sinatra, "I wanted to do it my way." Furthermore, I was allowed to choose the staff for the bank.

I felt comfortable with the current business environment and confident that some of my past banking customers would bring business to the new bank. Gerald had now lined up several potential investors. Some of my family members and a business partner, Ronnie Hammond, also became investors in the bank. I knew that my business reputation was at risk, and I later felt the pressure in trying to fulfill everyone's expectations.

On July 14, 2004, the organizers held an investor meeting at Eagles Landing Country Club. Gerald had asked me to speak on the merits of starting a new bank. I told those in attendance that banks were vital to their respective communities. Banks, historically, were good investments for their shareholders. As long as Henry County continued to grow and real estate values remained constant, the bank should reach profitability in a few years. I informed the group that the best approach in maximizing earning goals was to concentrate on real estate related lending. My previous experience had shown that these types of loans offered the least amount of risk. The investors were enthusiastic and expressed their desire to proceed. They assigned the responsibility of exploring banking opportunities to Gerald and me.

I knew the process of starting a new bank would be long, arduous, and complicated. The first order of business was to seek legal assistance. The organizers engaged John McGoldrick of Martin Snow, LLP to assist in the legal process. John was a partner in a law firm in Macon that represented many community banks. John suggested the group first consider the purchase of an existing bank rather than pursuing a new bank charter. The obvious advantage was the ability to conduct business immediately. It was a logical alternative to the time-consuming and expensive stock offering route. I had been acquainted with the organizers of FirstCity and High Trust who had purchased small South Georgia banks. Both were able to receive approval to relocate their bank headquarters to the Eagles Landing area in Stockbridge.

The search for a bank took us in several directions. Gerald and I visited a bank in Monroe where the bank's owner and president had recently died. His son had inherited controlling interest and wanted to sell his bank. An impasse was reached early on as the seller did not wish to relinquish the CEO's role. Some members of the group met several times with the directors of Community National Bank in Ashburn. They were anxious to sell their bank after a new branch in St. Mary's, Georgia, had saddled them with heavy loan losses. Their bank, however, was a bit too large and too expensive to fit our budget. On another occasion Gerald and I flew to Tarpon Springs, Florida, to look at a small bank that was also having some financial difficulty. Its headquarters was in an oversized converted warehouse building. One would think that being across the street from a Catholic Church; it would have utilized the spiritual help that was available next door. Being a Florida bank, however, eliminated any chance to branch in Georgia. The organizers concluded that none of these banks offered a suitable investment opportunity.

Gerald and I learned of a small bank in Abbeville named the Dorsey State Bank that was looking for an investor. The Bank was located in South Georgia about a two-hour drive from McDonough. The majority ownership was vested in two brothers, James and Glenn Dorsey. They had inherited the control of the bank from Nina Dorsey. Glenn, who resided in Abbeville, assumed the management duties of the bank. Although he had a limited banking background, Glenn, with the help of the staff quickly learned bank operations and lending. From Glenn's knowledge of Abbeville, he was able to retain and grow a loyal customer base. Unlike the other banks visited, the purchase of Dorsey State Bank showed the greatest promise.

Wilcox County had five banks with seven offices. Two of the offices were in Abbeville. Dorsey State Bank had approximately 6% of the county's deposits according to available data.[1]

WILCOX COUNTY BANKS

FDIC Insured Banks	Locations	Deposits ($) (000)	Market Share
Colony Bank Wilcox	Rochelle Pineview	43,551	36%
Wilcox County Bank	Rochelle Abbeville	34,695	29%
Planters First	Pineview	19,682	16%
Rochelle State Bank	Rochelle	14,971	13%
Dorsey State Bank	Abbeville	7,348	6%
Total		$12,0247	100%

Abbeville was situated in Wilcox County which bordered the Ocmulgee River. It was a typical South Georgia town with only one traffic light. Its economy relied primarily on agriculture and timber. Its largest employer was a state prison that served as a medium security facility for the State's felons. The 2,298 residents in the city included the 1,827 inmate population. The bank was located within sight of the prison. I was relieved to learn that there had been only one unsuccessful jail break in the history of the prison. If one was hungry, there was a place called Ophelia's that specialized in good fried chicken. Abbeville was the county seat, but the better-known towns in the area were Rochelle, Hawkinsville, Fitzgerald, and Cordele. If one took Exit 99 off of I-75 and could avoid the logging trucks, it was a 30-minute ride to Abbeville. Wilcox

County was famous for its large population of wild hogs and celebrated the distinction with its Ocmulgee Wild Hog Festival.

After a visit to Abbeville and spending an afternoon with Glenn Dorsey, Gerald and I were convinced that Dorsey State Bank offered a realistic opportunity to own a bank. The discussions continued with James Dorsey, who was an attorney in Atlanta. Not knowing what to expect from an Atlanta attorney, I found Jim to be very pleasant and courteous. The negotiations proved fruitful ending in a tentative agreement. With the investor's consent, we entered into a Letter of Intent, which was executed on April 23, 2004.

The Dorsey family were the most prominent business leaders in Abbeville. They had owned the local car dealership, funeral home, and the bank. John H. Dorsey founded the Dorsey Banking Company in October 1925 and managed its operation until his death in 1951. Jake Dorsey managed the bank until 1959. Nina Dorsey followed until her retirement in 1985 and turned the helm over to her son, Glenn. He wore two hats as he was also the local Magistrate Judge. He performed a marriage ceremony at the Courthouse in the morning and then financed the couple's honeymoon at the bank in the afternoon. Glenn and James, who were in their sixties, had begun to plan their retirement.

The Dorseys chose to keep their bank private even after Roosevelt created the FDIC in 1933. In 1976, however, the successors obtained a state bank charter, which transferred supervision to the Georgia Department of Banking and Finance and the FDIC. The change meant that the deposits were now insured by the Deposit Insurance Fund. The new name for the bank was Dorsey State Bank. The long-standing institution had survived the Great Depression and for over 80 years had provided the financial needs for the citizens in Abbeville and Wilcox County. At that time, Dorsey State Bank, based on its deposit size, was the smallest established commercial bank in Georgia.

Thus, began the "due diligence period" ...where the organizers determined the true financial condition of the bank. It was determined that Donnie Luker from Mauldin & Jenkins would prepare a feasibility study and value assessment of the bank. Mauldin & Jenkins was the predominant accounting firm for Georgia community banks and eventually became the Bank's auditor and tax accountant. Donnie surmised that the bank charter in itself was worth 1.6 times the bank's book value. In Dorsey State Bank's case, that was approximately $1.6 million. I reviewed all of Dorsey State Bank's loans, which totaled only $3.8 million. At the end of 2004, Dorsey State Bank had approximately $7.9 million in total assets which included $6.9 million in deposits. Its shareholder equity (net worth) was just under $1 million, and its net income for 2004 was $79,322. I did not find any meaningful loan problems or operation issues.

Donnie prepared a pro forma forecasting the probable growth and profitability of Dorsey State Bank with the injection of additional capital. The five-year pro forma, as detailed in the balance sheet and income statement, projected the bank to reach $100 million in assets and earn $550 thousand by the end of the fifth year.[2] From the encouraging numbers, Gerald and I recommended to the investors to allow us to proceed with the purchase.

The first step was to create a corporate entity that could acquire a bank. On July 26, 2004, the organizers incorporated Enterprise Banking Company Inc., a Holding Company for that purpose. It was agreed to rename the bank from Dorsey State Bank to Enterprise Banking Company. The organizers became the initial corporate directors: Gerald Hudgins, Chairman; Hans Broder, President; Randy Mahaffey, Vice President; Sonny Sprayberry, Secretary; and Hugh Morton, Treasurer. These individuals were the initial investors and became the Board's executive committee.

DORSEY STATE BANK
Five Year Plan | Probable Case Projection

BALANCE SHEET	($) (000)				
ASSETS	12/31/05	12/31/06	12/31/07	12/31/08	12/31/09
Cash	3,701	7,826	10,466	11,772	13,170
Investments	242	595	1,564	3,432	5,424
Loans	4,132	15,771	30,516	54,253	76,410
Reserve	-104	-237	-305	-543	-764
Building & Equipment	216	1,707	2,639	2,534	2,432
Other	104	504	904	1,304	1,704
Total Assets	8,291	26,166	45,784	72,752	98,376
LIABILITIES & EQUITY					
Deposits	7,348	16,166	35,564	62,238	87,133
Other Liabilities	42	442	842	1,242	1,642
Total Liabilities	7,390	16,608	36,406	63,480	88,775
Common Stock	0	10,700	10,700	10,700	10,700
Retained Earnings	901	-1,142	-1,322	-1,427	-1,099
Total Equity	901	9,558	9,378	9,273	9,601
Total Liabilities & Equity	8,291	26,166	45,784	72,752	98,376
INCOME STATEMENT					
Interest Income	481	768	1,729	3,130	4,798
Interest Expense	152	260	599	1,153	1,761
Net Interest Income	329	508	1,130	1,977	3,037
Provisions for Loan Loss		149	105	302	313
Other Income	77	41	94	170	261
Operating Expenses	330	743	1,299	1,949	2,436
Net Income	76	-343	-181	-105	548

....

In choosing a name for the corporation, the Board and the committee considered various non-traditional bank names. The final list was narrowed to six choices. The choices were Keystone Banking Company,

Keystone State Bank, Enterprise Banking Company, Enterprise State Bank, Benchmark Banking Company, and Benchmark State Bank. After discussion the Board chose Enterprise Banking Company. It was determined that the "entrepreneurial spirit" connotation in the name best described the background of the investors and established the theme for the bank's business plan. My daughter, Mia, designed the logo. The name change occurred at Abbeville on May 1, 2005.

In order to finance the purchase of the bank, I contacted The Bankers Bank (TBB). With my former ties, I was familiar with The Banker Bank's policy concerning bank acquisition loans. I knew it had assisted other community bankers in this regard. All of the future Board members seeking loans had strong financial statements. Each was capable of making a 25% down payment toward the purchase. Ann Cross, the Senior Lender, provided loan commitments utilizing the borrower's bank stock as collateral. With the financing in place, the borrowing investors closed their loans with TBB on March 23, 2005.

That day, five investors borrowed funds from The Bankers Bank. I borrowed a sizable amount using my shares in Dorsey State Bank and Henry County Bancshares, Inc. as collateral. I used a portion of my 401k and other savings to make the down payment. I had approximately 23% stake in the new Bank. Later I acquired some additional shares to where my ownership reached nearly 25%.

The next day the investors completed the purchase of Dorsey State Bank by paying the existing five shareholders of Dorsey State Bank $1,700,000 which represented 90% ownership in the Bank. In exchange for the remaining 10% interest in Dorsey State Bank, the existing shareholders received 10% of the new shares in Enterprise Banking Company, Inc. The company initially issued 25,000 shares of common stock and established an acquisition price per share of $475.56. The seventeen new shareholders invested $8,900,000 into the company. The new capital added to the existing capital already at Dorsey State Bank less the organizational costs bought the total capitalization to approximately $9,700,000. The infusion of cash gave birth to Enterprise Banking Company.

Enterprise Banking Company | Abbeville, GA | 2005

CHAPTER TWO

THE BOARD OF DIRECTORS

Our first task was the election of the Boards. Three of the existing Dorsey State Bank Board members were assigned to serve on the Advisory Board for Enterprise Banking Company. They were James (Jim) Dorsey, Glenn Dorsey and Charles Cannon. The regular monthly Advisory Board meetings were held in Abbeville. Bob Greene, Bobby Hudgins, Gerald Hudgins and I were added to the Advisory Board. Later Jim Dorsey resigned and was replaced by Blake Hudgins. Glenn Dorsey continued to manage the Abbeville office as President and CEO. The other two existing Dorsey State Bank Board members, Jim Dorsey and Richard Willingham, were elected to the regular Bank Board in McDonough. The Directors in McDonough served on the Boards of both the Holding Company and Bank.

All of the Directors were well qualified as they had business and/or banking backgrounds. All would become committed to the long-term success of the company. To each I held with utmost respect. Although I was given a great deal of latitude in managing the Bank, I was very transparent with my decisions. We worked closely as a team.

In addition to each Director's success in business they all had interesting backgrounds. Education wise, four of the Directors graduated from Georgia Tech, two from Georgia State, one from Clemson, one from Tulane and I would be the lone UGA alum. All of the Directors were either former bankers or bank directors with the exception of Gerald. As a result of his many real estate ventures and the need to finance them, Gerald was acquainted with a network of bankers and had knowledge of real estate lending. The director group included a practicing attorney in Jim Dorsey.

Upon my graduation from UGA, I was fortunate to land a teaching position at Stockbridge High School. I was one of three business education teachers and taught typing and business-related courses. When the school's librarian invited Lyndy and I to have lunch with the President of First State, my career path changed direction. With a Swiss heritage, the career move was probably driven by fate as I was destined to become a banker. First State was only a $6 million bank when I joined the company in 1971. When senior management left for other opportunities, I was able to convince the Board to name me as its next President and CEO in 1976. During my tenure I had the satisfaction of witnessing the bank's growth and maturation as a financial institution. With 25 years as CEO of First State, I knew what was required to be a profitable bank. I had the support of a well-qualified and knowledgeable team to manage and oversee the Bank. I would serve as CEO and President.

Gerald Hudgins was the Chairman. Gerald was one of Henry County's largest and most successful builder-developers and the owner of several related companies. He and his companies can take credit for developing some 75 subdivisions in the area and building 1200 homes. Gerald had been a customer of First State, and over the years he had become a personal friend and business partner. Though his successes were in residential and commercial real estate, Gerald was able to purchase several South Georgia farms. At one time his farm operations included 2,000 head of Black Agnus cattle. His business contacts in South Georgia proved to be beneficial in attracting new customers to the Abbeville office.

In 2013 the *Henry Herald* published an article entitled "Henry businessman a pillar of the community." As a business and community

HENRY HERALD January 30, 2013

Henry Businessman a pillar of the community

By: Jeylin White

When you hear the name Gerald Hudgins around Henry County there's usually one word that's associated with it "generous."

Hudgins has owned Apple Realty for more than 30 years in Henry County. He said he has worked closely with Henry County Board of Education and during the late 90's he donated computers to local middle schools to assist with launching a pilot program. Hudgins also helped fund an SAT and ACT prep-program for high school students looking to achieve a higher score on their pre-college test exams. In addition, the Chairperson for the Henry County Chamber of Commerce also donated the land for the new building, just to name a few.

Hudgins said he lives by the biblical motto: "it is better to give than it is to receive." He said business was successful, which gave him the ability to donate generously.

....

leader Gerald was recognized for his generosity.[3]

Randy Mahaffey was the Vice Chairman. Randy was CEO of Ply Mart, Inc., a family owned building supply company. At that time Ply Mart, Inc. had 33 stores in Georgia. At its peak the Ply Mart stores were generating a million dollars in sales per month. Randy's claim to fame was athletics. At 6' 7", he was a star basketball player for Clemson and was drafted in the second round by the L.A. Lakers. He chose to play in the short-lived ABA for the Kentucky Colonels, who had also drafted him. In his rookie season, he was named as an ABA All-Star. He was traded to the New York Nets and later to the Carolina Cougars. He and his three older brothers hold the all-time record for points scored by brothers at one university (Clemson).

Hugh Morton was the Treasurer. Hugh was the owner of Peachtree Homes and was building over 100 houses per year in his glory days. As a former banker of 16 years, he was CEO of Home Federal and Chief Lending Officer at Southern Federal. Hugh played football for Tulane.

THE ATLANTA JOURNAL-CONSTITUTION March 3, 2013
"The key to life is persistence"

Homebuilder Hugh Morton has battled cancer, climbed "The Seven Summits" and wrestled with the housing meltdown. You may be surprised to find out which was the toughest fight.

By: Henry Unger

One of the hardest things in life is learning how to overcome obstacles.

Hugh Morton, president of Jonesboro-based Peachtree Homes, has faced three though ones — climbing to the top of the highest mountain peaks on each of the seven continents, trying to withstand the recent housing crisis as a homebuilder, and fighting cancer.

By the time Morton reached his last summit – Vinson Massif in Antarctica in 1999 – fewer than 70 people in the world had climbed "The Seven Summits". Morton endured minus – 40 degrees temperatures, severe winds, and the sight of three people frozen in the snow who died trying.

Most of his climbs were made while he was running a homebuilding company that thrived when metro Atlanta grew rapidly in the 1990s and first half of the 2000s. But the collapse of real estate market starting in 2007 turned black ink into red, forcing Morton to decide between bailing out or repaying mountains of debt with money he didn't have. While wrestling with that issue, he was diagnosed with lymphoma.

I got in to hiking when I was in the Boy Scouts. When I was 39, I went on a trek to the base camp of Mt. Everest and I got captivated by it. I came back with the notion that I wanted some time to climb. Something in me kept pushing toward the goal of climbing seven summits.

Hugh Morton has climbed the highest mountains peak on each the seven continents.

Kilimanjaro, Africa (Tanzania) 19,340 ft. | 1988

McKinley, North American (Alaska) 20,320 ft. | 1989

Everest, Asia (Nepal) 29,035 ft. | 1992

Aconcagua, South America (Argentina) 22,834 ft. | 1995

Elbrus, Europe (Russia) 18,510 ft. | 1998

Kosciusko, Australia 7,310 ft. | 1998

Vinson Massif, Antarctica 16,066 ft. | 1999

His hobby was mountain climbing. He has the distinction of success-fully scaling the highest peaks in all seven continents including Mt. Everest, as well as the Matterhorn. I had the occasion to take a cable car to the base of the Matterhorn in Switzerland to see first-hand how difficult the upper section of the mountain was to scale.

Hugh was also an author. He wrote *The Big Gamble* in 1980 about the dangers of the "fair tax". His best work was entitled *The Great American Housing Fiasco*, an inside view of the mortgage crisis. *The Atlanta Journal and Constitution* (AJC) featured a story about Hugh Morton in March 2013. A summary of the article told of his three major challenges.[4]

Sonny Sprayberry was the Secretary. Sonny was a real estate agent and the President of Apple Realty. Sonny was Gerald's former brother-in-law, neighbor, and lifetime friend.

Gordon Skeen served as a Director. He was a retired banker of 25 years and a former commercial lender with First Union Bank, Decatur Federal, and Fulton Federal National Bank.

Robert Prather also served as a Director. He was the President of Gray Communications and former Director of First National Bank of Tucker. His company owned 17 television stations and numerous local newspapers. Gray Communications owned the *Henry Herald* and *Clayton Herald*. Bob served on numerous boards including Diebold, Rawlings Sporting Goods Company, and Bull Run. His seat on Victorinox Board, which manufactures the ubiquitous Swiss Army Knife in Switzerland, was the one that intrigued me. Bob had a chance to meet and get to know many well-known personalities. One of the more notable was the billionaire business magnate, Warren Buffet.

James Dorsey was a nephew of John Dorsey, the original founder of the Bank and was raised in Abbeville. He graduated from Georgia Tech and obtained his law degree from the University of Virginia. He was a partner with Arnall Golden Gregory LLP, law firm of Atlanta. In addition to being named as a Director, Jim was Chairman of American Southern Bank in Kennesaw. He is a Vietnam veteran and retired as a Commander from the Navy Reserves.

Richard Willingham filled the last seat on the Board. Richard was a businessman from Rochelle. He owned an insurance company, and his Refuse and Recycling business served Wilcox County.

Richard served until May 2006. Jim Henderson was elected to the Board in May 2009. Jim was a prominent businessman and former Director of the Bank of Hampton and Bank of Griffin. He began his career with J. M. Tull Company in Atlanta, Georgia, and was a founder and one of the three principals in J & J, Inc., a manufacturer and a wholesaler of nickel alloy fittings, pipes, and rods.

Early on, the Board made some key corporate decisions. The Board elected to organize the Holding Company as a Subchapter S Corporation for tax purposes. With the approval of the Subchapter S designation by the IRS, the tax liability was passed directly to the shareholders via a K-1. Corporate income or loss was reported on the individual shareholder's 1040 tax return. There was no secondary tax on the distribution of dividends as is the case with regular C Corporations. To qualify for this tax status, the corporation could have no more than 100 shareholders, and each shareholder had to be "accredited". To be deemed "accredited", a shareholder had to have a certain level of income and net worth. The shareholders for the most part were a mixture of well-to-do individuals. The group included a doctor, a judge, farmers, builders, realtors, developers, and a sundry of successful businessmen and businesswomen.

The path from the purchase of Dorsey State Bank to having the headquarters relocated to McDonough was a complicated process. With the aid of our attorneys, Mike White and John McGoldrick, Enterprise began the preparation of various applications to the Banking Department, FDIC, Federal Reserve, and Securities and Exchange Commission. The bank policies were my responsibility. The Dorsey State Bank policies required updating and/or rewriting before submission to the regulators. Those included the Loan, Investment, Capital, Liquidity, Personnel, Consumer

Compliance, Asset-Liability, and Internal Audit, to name a few. All of the Directors were required to receive regulatory approval before being allowed to serve. Criminal background checks, finger prints, and credit histories were obtained. I am happy to report that everyone passed and was approved. The Board appointed various members to serve on the Loan, Audit, Asset & Liability, and Personnel Committees.

I began searching for a management staff for the new Bank. The hiring of senior officers including President, Senior Lender, and CFO, also required regulatory scrutiny and approval. I was able to hire Ray Nipper, a South Georgia banker now living in McDonough as Senior Lender. Keith Jackson served as CFO. Karen Cooper, the daughter of Sam Parrish and one-time CEO at First State and my former boss, was employed as the Commercial Loan Officer.

The founding directors adopted a business plan as of September 1, 2004 that became the footprint and game plan for the Bank. The Business Plan was similar to those of the other area community banks. Several of the Directors attended a "Director College" sponsored by the Community Bankers Association. Over several days, the Directors were instructed on the duties and responsibilities of bank directors. One of the speakers was the FDIC's economist. He warned of the impending real estate bubbles that would be occurring in certain western and northern states. The new Directors were pleased to learn from his prediction that the Atlanta area would be spared. Because of Atlanta's favorable climate, its economic strength, and the lower cost of housing, the Atlanta area in all likelihood would avoid a real estate downturn. The appropriate regulatory agencies approved the business plan, bank policies, management team, and headquarter relocation from Abbeville to McDonough.

CHAPTER THREE

MEET THE REGULATORS

In the Broadway play and later the movie "The Damn Yankees", a baseball fan, Joe Boyd, agrees to sell his soul to the devil if the Washington Senators could only beat the Yankees. Bank boards and management would likewise be at the mercy of a higher power, namely the regulators. To the officers and staff, regulators were a nemesis. In a typical Enterprise "Safety and Soundness" audit, various examiners were on site for three weeks. Bank personnel were expected to be on standby to fetch files and answer questions. Their visit was an interruption to the daily routine, and their departure was always welcomed. But, without regulators and regulations providing oversight and direction, the banking industry would be in a state of chaos.

In addition to approving the purchase of Dorsey State Bank and the formation of Enterprise Banking Company, the Georgia Department of Banking and Finance[5] (Banking Department) was the primary agency that oversaw the Bank. The Banking Department shared regulatory responsibility for Georgia state-chartered financial institutions with federal counterparts, the Federal Deposit Insurance Corporation and Federal Reserve Bank.

The Banking Department was established in 1919 by the Georgia General Assembly and through the years saw its powers broadened and its application process streamlined. The objective of the Banking Department was summarized in its Mission Statement...to promote safe, sound, competitive financial services in Georgia through its regulation and supervision. The Banking Department charged the institutions an annual fee based on the institution's asset size. The Banking Department strived to reduce the regulatory burdens on its regulatory entities; however, such efforts were not always apparent to the bankers.

The Federal Deposit Insurance Corporation[6] (FDIC) was created by Congress in 1933 to maintain stability and public confidence in the nation's banking system that was in shambles after the Great Depression. In addition to its role as insurer, the FDIC was the primary federal regulator of federally insured state-chartered banks that were not members of the Federal Reserve System which included Enterprise. The FDIC also acted as receiver for insured depository institutions that failed. The FDIC defined its supervision program as one that encompassed activities undertaken to promote safe and sound banking operations while complying with fair lending, consumer protection, and other applicable statutes and regulations.

When an insured depository institution failed, the FDIC was ordinarily appointed receiver. In that capacity, it assumed responsibility for recovering funds from the disposition of the receivership's assets and the pursuit of the receivership's claims. The funds that were collected from the sale of assets and the disposition of valid claims would be distributed to the receivership's creditors. The FDIC maintained that the receiverships were managed to maximize net return and would be terminated in an orderly and timely manner. Potential recoveries, including claims against professionals, would be investigated and resolved in a fair and cost-effective manner.

The FDIC maintained the Deposit Insurance Fund (DIP) by assessing depository institutions an insurance premium. FDIC deposit insurance was backed by the full faith and credit of the United States government should the fund become depleted. Accordingly, the resources of the United States government stood behind FDIC-insured depositors. Bank failures typically represented a cost to the DIF because the FDIC, as receiver of the failed institution, would liquidate assets that may have declined substantially in value while, at the same time, making good on the institution's deposit obligations.

In 1913 Congress created the Federal Reserve[7] (Fed) as the central banking system of the United States. The Fed would have three main functions: provide and maintain an effective payments system, supervise and regulate banking operations, and conduct monetary policy. Its sphere of influence related more to the national economy and financial service needs of the large banks. Enterprise relied on correspondent banks for such service and did not become a member of the Fed. But, with the existence of Enterprise Banking Company, Inc. (bank holding company) as owner of Enterprise Banking Company (Bank), it was regulated by the Fed. The organizers formed the holding company so that the Bank could offer other non-bank services through separate entities such as an Insurance Agency, Mortgage Company, Finance Company, or other related financial businesses, if it so desired. Banks in themselves were not allowed to own such subsidies. Since Enterprise was strictly a bank operation, its holding company, Enterprise Banking Company, Inc., required little oversight. Therefore, the annual Fed examination was conducted online as an accounting audit and not via a physical visit.

The three named regulators carried out their duties through foot soldiers called bank examiners. These individuals audited the banking activities and were charged with determining the health status of Enterprise. To become an examiner required a 4-year undergraduate degree with a strong background in accounting and finance. As per the 2015 U.S. Bureau of Labor Statistics, the bank examiner was modestly paid and had advancement opportunities in position and salary. Applicants were tested for aptitude, and once employed had continuous training throughout their careers.[8]

Not everyone was cut out to be an examiner. It took a specific personality trait to work in a bureaucratic environment pouring through tons of records, traveling from one bank to another, and writing numerous reports. According to Jung's and Briggs Myers' theory of personality[9], an examiner was described as an "ISTJ" personality type. The characteristics of an "ISTJ" type was said to have been Introvert-Sensing-Thinking-Judging. These were people who enjoyed working alone or in small groups at a calculated speed. They were pragmatic people who tended to focus on the facts and had strong opinions about the way things should be done. These were individuals who had a passion for finding fault...sometimes it appeared that they would search until they found one.

As for bankers the personality type was "ESTP". This personality type was defined as an Extrovert-Sensor-Thinker-Perceiver. These individuals worked better in crisis situations and enjoyed working with people. They were practical and open-minded persons who were able to act on a dime and were willing to be flexible. They possessed people skills and strived to accommodate those in need.

Each was well suited for handling the specific tasks put before them. But, with different personality traits it was easy to surmise that bankers and examiners had conflicting agendas. That was certainly the case at Enterprise. The State examiners were considered to be firm but fair and would provide constructive criticism. The FDIC examiners were generally stricter and at times overly critical of minor issues. It should be noted, that no bank failure can be blamed on the examiners or the regulatory agencies. During this stressful time, regulatory agencies, examiners, and bank regulations tended to create apprehension and doubt in the minds of management and the board. Past decisions were second guessed, and future decisions were made with fingers crossed.

One of the more frustrating changes in banking has been the emergence of consumer protection laws. Ralph Nader, a political activist and attorney, should be credited for the government reforms in consumer protectionism. His 1965 publication, *Unsafe at Any Speed*[10], questioned the safety record of American automobiles. His efforts led to the overhaul of the Federal Trade Commission and brought about new laws for the auto manufacturers. The trend moved to the banking industry in 1968 with the Truth in Lending Act. From there, the onslaught of new regulations continued unabated. As a result, I saw the introduction of hundreds of compliance regulations during my banking career.

Community banks have full-time Compliance Officers to ensure, that management adhere to the existing compliance laws. At Enterprise, the Compliance Officer spent time tracking continual changes. Management was always bracing for the next round of new regulations. The Compliance Officer attended quarterly seminars to receive continuing education. His duties included regular reporting to the various regulatory agencies. Compliance had become an integral part of bank personnel's interaction with customers. As a result of the electronic age, new accounts and loans were created and processed through the Modern Banking's computer program. An outside service was responsible for the accuracy of the banking forms. The staff witnessed the continual change in the structure and language of the forms that were necessitated by new and revised compliance regulations.

Since non-compliance presented a sizable risk to banks in possible lawsuits and penalties, regulators performed separate audits of the bank's compliance programs. Many of the consumer protection laws were needed, but the sheer number had gotten out of control. When home purchasers arrived at their mortgage closing, they were shocked with the number of loan documents that they were expected to read, understand, and sign. The "deed to secure debt" alone exceeded twelve pages. In earlier times two pages was sufficient for the bank to perfect it's lien. The burden was on the lender to dot every "I" and cross every "T", if it expected to prevail in its litigations against borrowers, who had defaulted on their notes.

CHAPTER FOUR

EARLY YEARS OF ENTERPRISE

Our management team consisting of Karen Cooper, Ray Nipper, and myself began banking operations from office space provided by Gerald Hudgins in his McDonough office building. Gerald provided the desks and furnishings for the temporary Bank. Management was able to acquire some basic office equipment. The staff was now able to process its paperwork and transactions through the Abbeville office. The McDonough Officers were making loans and opening accounts electronically. Nevertheless, I was making regular trips to Abbeville, spending the nights at a hunting lodge in Arabi belonging to Bob Greene, one of the Abbeville directors. I remember how quiet and peaceful the bunk house was without the interstate noise or sirens, even the birds seem to whisper. When making my morning runs, the only traffic I encountered was an occasional tractor. The new business coming out of McDonough energized the Abbeville staff. The Bank was off and running.

The management team had to decide between three options to handle the Bank's data processing function. The first option was to use an external data processor that could process the computer work off site. The Bank would pay a monthly fee for the service, but would forgo the purchase cost of the hardware and software. The second option was to acquire new hardware, software, and an operating system from a vendor located in the Atlanta area and process in-house. The third option was to remain with the existing system already in-house and utilize the bookkeeping personnel at Abbeville. Management elected to stay with

Abbeville's in-house data processing system, Modern Banking Systems (MBS). The upfront costs were limited to the new equipment needed for the McDonough office. MBS provided the hardware and training.

The management team, along with Glenn Dorsey, flew to Jackson, Mississippi, to get a crash course on how to use the program. The MBS program was not as sophisticated as the Jack Henry operating system which I had been accustomed to while at First State. I would not have called their MBS system "modern", but it was adequate, less expensive, and suitable for a small bank. The decision pleased the Abbeville personnel since they were already comfortable with the system. The Abbeville office was performing the bookkeeping function...why make a change. As the volume of transactions increased, the Bank was later forced to renovate the second floor of the Abbeville office to expand its bookkeeping operations.

In order to achieve the growth and profitability goals, it was important to focus on lending. Stiff competition among the banks and the emergence of credit unions had reduced service charge income from checking accounts and other bank services. The once reliable income producers became non-existent. Free-checking had become the norm in financial institutions. Income from securities and overnight federal funds historically had always been a staple for bank earnings. Now, these too were on the decline. On the bright side, there existed a tremendous appetite for loans, primarily real estate related loans. Banking regulations set the lending limit a bank can lend a borrower. Collateralized loan(s) in aggregate could not to exceed 25% of the bank's capital. With the injection of $10 million in capital, Enterprise could lend up to $2.5 million to one borrower...a sizable amount for a small bank. In the midst of the housing boom, the builders, developers, and real estate investors were the most frequent seekers of loans. Since the cost of real estate in the area was at an all-time high, many of the loan requests were large. The Bank's loan portfolio grew rapidly.

It was quite a shock to the bookkeeping staff in Abbeville, as they were asked to process loans from $500,000 to $2,000,000. Prior to that time the largest loan that Dorsey State Bank had made was $50,000. Wilcox County seldom had more than a few new housings starts in a given year. So, few, that the county had no meaningful building codes, zoning requirements, or construction inspections. Whereas, Henry County was having over 2,000 new housing starts per year.

McDonough Officers were comfortable in the Hudgins Building but needed a more permanent setting. The Board approved the purchase of 1.8 acres at a price of $750,000. The property was located at the intersection of Georgia Highway 20 and Westridge Boulevard, two miles west of Interstate 75 and six miles east of the Atlanta Motor Speedway and adjoining Henry County Airport. The Board considered the site as a prime location with CVS, Publix, and Wachovia across the street. Walgreens had previously paid $1.6 million for an adjacent corner. The Hudgins Building, Henry County Chamber of Commerce, Regions Bank, and Henry Water Authority were our neighbors. Gerald was able to have the street behind the Bank named "Enterprise Parkway".

Later, the Board learned of a modular bank building that was available in Carrollton, Georgia. The building belonged to McIntosh Commercial Bank, a new bank that had just completed the construction of its new bank building. After inspecting the modular office, the Board determined the structure to be an ideal temporary facility. The modular bank was purchased for $75,000 and transported from Carrollton to Enterprise Parkway in December 2005. The building would be located adjacent to the commercial lot the Board had purchased. The facility was fully equipped with drive-up window, night depository, money vault and furniture. Enterprise now had its own banking office.

By the end of 2005, Enterprise had grown to $21 million in assets,

$11 million in deposits, $11 million in loans, $10 million in capital, and earned $73 thousand. The Bank held its first Shareholder meeting on May 12, 2006. The Board and Shareholders were pleased with the Bank's progress. In spite of one-time start-up costs, Enterprise was profitable in its first year.

On August 15, 2005, the Bank had its first examination by the Banking Department. The Safety and Soundness audit was conducted in Abbeville. The Banking Department and the FDIC would alternate the duties of conducting the regular Safety and Soundness examinations. The Banking Department gave Enterprise high marks in all areas. Later, the FDIC conducted an Internal Technology (I.T.) Exam and a Compliance Exam. The parent company, Enterprise Banking Company, Inc., also had its first periodic examination by the Fed. It seemed that an examination team was either coming or going during the entire time of the Bank's existence.

Growing quickly, historically, had been difficult for a new "stand alone" bank. A bank could only lend up to 75% of its deposits with its deposits coming from its local trade area. Through the magic of Internet banking, a bank was able to obtain deposits from anywhere in the U.S. These were called Brokered Deposits. A Brokered Deposit was a pool of $100,000 to $250,000 Certificates of Deposit. These C.D.s were insured by the FDIC and generally priced at a lower rate than the same C.D.s offered in the Henry County market. The use of Brokered C.D.s had saved Enterprise approximately 25 basis points, (one-fourth of one percent) in interest cost. Enterprise also borrowed from the Federal Home Loan Bank to fund its loans. In May 2006 the Banking Department approved the Enterprise's use of Brokered Deposits provided their aggregate did not exceed 35% of total deposits.

Banks like many businesses operated on margins. A typical community bank was said to have a successful year if it had a rate of return

(ROA) of 1% of its assets. Therefore, it was imperative for a new bank to achieve a certain size, before it could sustain profitability. The major expense for a bank was the cost of funds which were the deposits. This cost was market driven. Next was the personnel cost, a fixed expense. Too little staff would compromise the quality of the service, it could offer. The third largest expense was the occupancy cost, which included the building and related expenses. Based on the initial operating projections, the Bank would have to reach $75 million in assets before it could achieve a break-even point. Although Enterprise had already reached a degree of profitability, it would be more difficult to have consist earnings, once the Bank felt the impact of its new building. The Bank needed to grow and to achieve this goal, Management needed to increase its loan and deposit business.

The focus during this period was generating income producing assets. With adequate sources of funding, the Loan Officers embarked on finding loans. As a new Bank, the objective was to target specific customers to build a loan portfolio of strong borrowers. The Board members and shareholders were excellent sources of referrals. The Board had adopted a thorough Loan Policy. The Policy assigned lending limits to each Officer and established Loan Committees to review and approve the larger credit lines. The McDonough Loan Committee met every two weeks while the Abbeville Loan Committee met once a month.

Loans that exceeded the Loan Officer's limits required the Committee's approval. The potential borrower was required to have a successful business track record, large net-worth, above average income, and sufficient collateral. The Loan Officer would assess the merits of the request by reviewing the borrower's loan application, personal and business financial statements, and tax returns. If the loan request passed the initial "smell test", the Loan Officer would proceed using some proven basic fundamentals to evaluate the borrower and the request. The ABC's of lending were called the "5 Cs of Credit"[11]. All lending personnel were schooled in the usage of these fundamentals. Although the 5 C's were more appropriate for consumer lending, some aspects also applied to commercial lending.

Character referred to the borrower's history for repaying debts. The Loan Officer would use Equifax to obtain an electronic credit report. The borrower's credit report would have detailed information about how much an applicant had borrowed in the past and whether he had repaid his loans on time. These reports also contained information on collection accounts, judgments, liens, and bankruptcies. The Fair Isaac Corporation (FICO) used this information to create a credit score, a snapshot of creditworthiness. The Better Business Bureau and Dunn and Bradstreet would provide information about the business. If the borrower's character was in question, there was no need to proceed any further.

Capacity measured a borrower's ability to repay a loan by comparing income against recurring debts and assessing the borrower's debt-to-income (DTI) ratio. In addition to examining income, the Loan Officer looked at the length of time an applicant had his business and/or had been at his job. Business and/or job stability were important.

Capital was considered to be the borrower's liquidity and ability to pay debt. The Loan Officer would analyze the borrower's personal financial statement and tax returns. In the case of a more complicated commercial loan, the Loan Officer would spread (analyze) the company's operating statements and balance sheets to determine the company's ability to service the debt.

Collateral, considered to be the most important, typically gave the assurance that if the borrower defaulted on the loan, the Bank then could sell the asset to recover the debt.

Conditions of the loan, such as the interest rate, terms, and amount requested would influence whether the loan was granted.

From the information gathered, the Loan Officer would then prepare a lengthy narrative that included the purpose of the loan, history of the borrower(s), financial analysis, discussion of the collateral, the ability to pay, sources of repayment, the strengths and weakness of the loan, and other details. He would organize the information in a summary report. The report and the financial data would become the loan package that would be presented to the Loan Committee and/or Board for approval. It was the responsibility of the Loan Officer to predetermine the risk and to present only loans that had merit. The final decision would be a group effort by all those involved in the decision-making process.

Once the loan was approved, every effort was made to determine the value of the collateral. The majority of Enterprise's loans were secured by real estate. Bank regulations required that banks obtain valuations of the real estate from outside appraisers. The appraisal was the Loan Officer's most important tool in determining if the Bank was properly margined... that there was sufficient equity in the collateral to secure the loan. The appraisal was performed by a licensed and/or certified appraiser.

An appraisal was an opinion or estimate of value. This opinion or estimate was derived by using three common approaches.[12]

The **cost approach** to determine value was to estimate the cost to replace or reproduce the improvements as of the date of the appraisal after deducting the physical deterioration, the functional obsolescence, and the economic obsolescence. The net amount was added to the cost of the land to reach a cost approach value. The fundamental premise of the cost approach was that a potential user of real estate would not or should not pay more for a property than it would cost to build an equivalent.

The **comparison approach** to determine value made use of other benchmark properties of similar size, quality, and location that had been recently sold. A comparison was made to the subject property and adjustments made to account for differences. A qualifying sale should be an arm's length transaction between a willing purchaser and a willing seller. The approach used a minimum of three recent sales of like property that were no more than six months old. The adjusted average of these sales established the market value.

The **income approach** to determine value was of primary importance in ascertaining the value of income producing properties. This approach provided an objective estimate of what a prudent investor would pay based upon the net income the property produced.

After thorough analysis of all general and specific data gathered from the three approaches, a final estimate or opinion of value was correlated. To the Loan Officer, the final evaluation or estimate should not have deviated too far from the cost to construct and to replace, if considered to be a reliable appraisal.

With an appraisal in hand, the Loan Officer would determine the maximum amount the Bank could lend. The Loan Officer would send instructions to the attorney to schedule a closing. The attorney or his agent would research the deed records at the courthouse in the county where the property was located to make sure there were no title defects. To ensure the Bank against future title claims, the borrower would be required to purchase Lender's Title Insurance. Title Insurance protected the Bank against a defect in the title such as challenges to ownership on unrecorded liens. The Loan Officer would then prepare the note and disclosure documents and send to the attorney. The attorney was then ready to close.

At this stage of the process, the Lending Committees had devoted a great deal of time diligently pouring through the information in the loan packages. All loans that were closed and funded by Enterprise were believed to be sound and were of acceptable risk. The borrowers had met the requirements, and the loans conformed to the existing Bank's loan policy requirements. But considering the eventual outcome of some of the loans, the Lenders could have used a Ouija board or read tea leaves and had better results.

While a board member for the Henry County Chamber of Commerce, I served on a committee that conducted an in-depth study of Henry County called "Henry Tomorrow". I learned from the data a great deal about demographic and economic trends in Henry County. One interesting statistic in the study was the growing number of small businesses in Henry County. Using this information, I encouraged the implementation of a marketing strategy that solicited new deposit accounts and loans from local business owners. The Loan Officers and New Account personnel also reached out to independent churches and farmers. These would be the priority contacts and, hopefully, would become the foundation of Enterprise's deposit base and loan portfolio. Witnessing the growth and success of a business had always been a rewarding experience for me. The development of mutual trust and confidence led to many long-standing banker/customer relationships.

Taking advantage of the booming housing market, the Loan Officers sought loans from small contractors/builders. These loans were short-term in nature and offered additional fee income. Traditionally, these borrowers were given a package of two or three residential construction loans. A solid sales contract or the payoff of an existing house led to a replacement construction loan. Loans to more established builders offered the opportunity to book large loans. These borrowers were high net worth individuals or companies, who had made a lot of money during the boom years. They were generally given lines of credit to be used to fund their real estate activities. These businesses had the wherewithal to build, sell, and finance their products. They had excellent track records and were sought after by all the banks.

Loans to speculators were the Bank's lowest priority. Although these borrowers were considered as minimal risk to the Bank, these relationships would be limited to a loan and seldom offered deposit accounts. These borrowers included groups of high income individuals, such as doctors, who wanted to make real estate investments. These borrowers could pay substantial amounts down toward the purchases and could service the payments from their personal incomes.

Henry County was experiencing a high degree of residential development. The urbanization movement was led by J. T. Williams, a CPA and developer from Tallahassee, Florida. He purchased an 1,800-acre tract located in and around the intersection of Hudson Bridge Road and I-75. Hudson Bridge Road was one of seven Henry County interstate interchanges and the only one that exited onto an unpaved road. Mr. Williams and his Killearn Companies converted the tract into what became Eagles Landing, a master planned community. Mr. Williams was instrumental in bringing a quality development to Henry County. His efforts attracted the attention of the metro area realtors and set in motion the influx of new residents. The interstate bridge was later named in his honor.

Various subdivisions followed appealing to the affordable, modest and upscale home buyers. The increased numbers of subdivisions that were in existence and under development had lengthened the absorption time for lot utilization by the builders. The normal six-month holding period for lots had increased to twenty-four months. Recognizing the negative trends, the Board shied away from new residential development loans. Instead, it preferred to make lot inventory loans in existing successful subdivisions, where the Bank could expect more predictable pay downs.

The Bank had the right fundamentals in place to build a loan portfolio. The Loan Officers were targeting the right borrowers. The Bank pursued the loan opportunities that were available at the time. These loans shaped the portfolio and later determined the destiny of the Bank. The loans that were being granted were to established borrowers who had adequate collateral and a solid credit background. When the Bank approved these loans, it assumed that the borrowers would be an acceptable risk.

The second examination of the Bank occurred after the relocation of Enterprise's headquarters to the modular office in McDonough. This audit was conducted by the FDIC in September of 2006. Again, the FDIC, as had the State, considered Enterprise to be well-capitalized and gave the Bank a satisfactory rating.

By the end of 2006, Enterprise had grown to $43 million in assets, $32 million in loans, $32 million in deposits, $10 million in capital, and had earned $332 thousand. The Bank had several individuals that had approached the Board about purchasing stock. The Board had a valuation of the Bank conducted in August of 2006. The consultant advised that the company stock was then worth $535 per share, a 12% increase over the initial per share price in March 2005. In 2006, ten new shareholders invested another $1 million in the company.

The list[13] identified the Enterprise shareholders, who owned the 26,870 shares of stock as of January 2011.

....

ENTERPRISE BANKING COMPANY, INC
2011 Shareholder List

Shareholder	Address	# of Shares	% of Ownership
Hans M. Broder, Jr.	Stockbridge	6,664	24.801%
Peter C. Broder	Atlanta	513	1.909%
Gerald W. Hudgins	McDonough	6,872	25.575%
Milton (Bobby) Hudgins	McDonough	210	0.782%
J.P. Hudgins	McDonough	210	0.782%
Randy Mahaffey	Norcross	3,145	11.705%
Hugh Morton	Jonesboro	1,097	4.083%

ENTERPRISE BANKING COMPANY, INC
2011 Shareholder List (cont.)

Shareholder	Address	# of Shares	% of Ownership
Bob Greene	Arabi	628	2.337%
Cindy M. Greene	Arabi	105	0.391%
Robert B. Greene	Arabi	210	0.782%
Carolyn P. Greene	Arabi	105	0.391%
M.B. Sprayberry, Jr.	Lilburn	524	1.950%
Robert S. Prather, Jr.	Atlanta	210	0.782%
Ronnie J. Hammond	Stockbridge	420	1.563%
Gordon Skeen	Atlanta	315	1.172%
Carey Bunn	Locust Grove	210	0.782%
Frankie Wilson	McDonough	210	0.782%
A. Glenn Dorsey	Abbeville	1,440	5.359%
James E. Dorsey	Sandy Springs	750	2.791%
Charles Cannon	Abbeville	285	1.061%
D. Warren Faircloth	Warner Robins	212	0.789%
Gordon Greene	Cordele	210	0.782%
Gerald B. Hudgins	McDonough	257	0.956%
Jeremy P. Crosby	McDonough	234	0.871%
Brandt Herndon	McDonough	187	0.696%
Shirley I. Crawford	Rebecca	187	0.696%
Thomas L. Gabey	McDonough	187	0.696%
Douglas R. Adams	McDonough	187	0.696%
James L. Henderson	Hampton	187	0.696%
Charles H. Renfroe	McDonough	187	0.696%
Patricia Anne Renfroe	McDonough	-	-
Charles Hugh Renfroe	McDonough	-	-
Michael Scott Renfroe	McDonough	-	-
Christa Renfroe Hurley	McDonough	-	-
John Edward Renfroe	McDonough	-	-

ENTERPRISE BANKING COMPANY, INC
2011 Shareholder List (cont.)

Shareholder	Address	# of Shares	% of Ownership
William M. Catoe, Jr.	Greenville, SC	275	1.023%
Larry E. Glenn	Lilburn	250	0.930%
Jo Ana Schine	Fayetteville	187	0.696%
Arbie Susanna Walker	Fayetteville	-	-
Madeline Rose Walker	Fayetteville	-	-
Molly Katherine Walker	Fayetteville	-	-
TOTAL		26,870	100.000%

The construction of the permanent office was an important endeavor as it was essential to present a positive image…one that reflected stability and permanency. The new facility would make it easier to attract new customers in a crowded banking market. Everyone was familiar with the Bank of Americas, Wachovias, and the SunTrusts. But, who had ever heard of Enterprise Banking Company? Once New Account Personnel and/or Loan Officers could get prospective customers in the door, it was felt that their patronage could be retained through the staff's attentiveness and service quality.

The Board approved a construction plan that was modest in design but would also accommodate future growth. The building was in a southern traditional style and very visible to passing motorists traveling on Hwy 20. It was a two-story brick structure with three drive-thru units.

During my banking career, I had witnessed other bankers, who had under and/or over-built their banking headquarters. With a vault full of money, it would be easy to build a "Taj Mahal" type structure. I questioned the wisdom of the Board of Directors of High Trust Bank and McIntosh Commercial Bank (bank buildings I had personally visited) who had approved the construction of large three-story facilities. McIntosh Commercial had spent $4.5 million on its building.

I was uneasy with the $1.6 million price tag for the new Enterprise building. In order to control costs, the Board elected not to install the elevator nor finish-out the second floor. The banking lobby was not overly spacious, instead all the Lending Officers had private offices that were accessible from the lobby. The facility was a comfortable and practically laid-out structure. With the additional capital, the Banking Department approved the construction of the permanent office. Operations in the new facility began June 2007.

Enterprise Banking Company | McDonough, GA | June 2007

During this period, the Board and I continued to be cost conscious. I had been accused from time to time of being a little miserly when it came time to spend the Bank's money. Employee salaries were in line or below industry standards. Expense accounts were closely monitored. The Bank did not purchase vehicles for staff usage or offer any special perks to employees. Board of Directors fees were limited to travel expenses which were $50 to $100 per month depending on the number of meetings. These were paid only while Enterprise was profitable. There were no bank-paid trips for Management or the Board members. Shareholder meetings were generally held in the main office lobby with little fanfare.

Our strategy to grow the loan portfolio was successful. By the end of 2007, Enterprise had grown to $62 million in assets, $47 million in loans, $50 million in deposits, and $11 million in capital and had earnings of $419 thousand. Interest spreads (margins) were favorable.

The Bank was meeting its expectations. The number of full-time employees now numbered 5 in Abbeville including Glen Dorsey, Jill McDuffie and Denise Howell and later Pearlie Cooper and Carolyn Wilcox and 11 in McDonough. The McDonough Office added Sandi Roberts as Senior Operations Officer and Randy Smith replaced Keith Jackson as CFO. Julie Coile as Loan Operations Officer, David Springer as Commercial Loan Officer, and Rhonda Foster as Mortgage Originator were now members of the staff. With the additional space, the Bank was able to move bookkeeping operations from Abbeville to McDonough. The Bank employed Tanya Lasseter, Tami Bell, and Stephanie Reed to help in the backroom operations. I hired a secretary named Arius Clark. I was pleased with my staff. The Bank was operating smoothly.

CHAPTER FIVE

2008 THE ADVENT OF CHANGE

At the end of 2007, Georgia had 334 banks.[14] Most had completed several consecutive quarters of increased earnings and were optimistic about their futures. Enterprise had just completed a successful year and was enjoying its new facility. The staff was busy opening new accounts and making loans, but the early signs of an economic slowdown were becoming apparent.

I knew that an economic slowdown was around the corner. I had experienced three such downturns during my banking career. The first recession occurred in the mid 1970s. The commercial real estate market in Atlanta had overheated creating vacancies and loan problems for the Atlanta banks. When it was rumored that Henry County would be the site of the second regional airport, investors flocked to the area and gobbled up the available land. The real estate boom came to a sudden end when the airport expansion did not materialize. Henry County struggled economically until the completion of I-75 in the late 1970s. The business development along its corridor rekindled the county's growth, and the local banks were able to recover with minimal damage.

The second downturn occurred in the early 1980s. Driven by high energy prices and runaway inflation, the nation's economy tanked. Lack of liquidity in the banking system resulted in unprecedented high interest rates. I recall the record high interest rates that benefited the savers but punished the borrowers. Cash strapped banks were paying 14% or more on short-term Certificates of Deposit (C.D.s) to maintain liquidity.

The loan interest rates had ranged between 18% to 22% for the desperate borrowers. Banks saw their overnight and short-term borrowings from the Federal Reserve Bank exceed 20%. Without working capital, businesses were struggling to survive.

The next local downturn occurred in the early 1990s with the bankruptcy of Eastern Airlines, the major employer on the southside, and the onset of the first Middle East War. The third recession was the shortest of the three and lasted only a couple of years.

During these recessions unemployment rose, and the housing market suffered. But, in all three cases the economy recovered and came back stronger than before. With such histories of recovery, it was thought that the next slowdown would follow the same pattern and would pose only a short-term threat to the local banks.

In 2008, Enterprise got its first taste of the broken mortgage system. The fallout began when pre-approved home buyers could no longer close on their purchases. The borrowers were deserted by their mortgage lenders, who could not find institutional investors to fund their mortgages. Enterprise had approved a construction line of credit for a builder, who was building and selling homes in the Porterdale area near the famous mill. The builder had experienced success in the subdivision. Enterprise had eagerly made him construction loans for his seven pre-sold houses. During the construction period, the mortgage underwriting requirements had stiffened and the availability of mortgage funding had evaporated. One of his houses did close, but the other closings fell through.

Unable to find new qualifying purchasers, the houses remained unsold. As a result, the builder began to struggle paying suppliers, subcontractors, and the Bank's interest. The subsequent loan defaults became Enterprise's first significant foreclosures. With some creative Enterprise financing arrangements, each house was eventually sold. The Bank wrote off approximately 25% of the amount loaned on each house. The foreclosures turned out to be a harbinger of things to come, as all builders began having difficulty moving their inventories.

In early 2008, Hugh Morton and I were on a guest panel that spoke to the Henry County Quality Growth Council members. The HCQG was an organization that a group including Gerald and I helped to create. The membership was composed of all those who were involved in the "growth business" namely builders, developers, real estate agents, and bankers. At that time HCQG had more than 200 members with Judy Neal and later Steve Cash as its full-time directors.

The topic of discussion was the future of the building business in Henry County. My comments to the audience included a prediction that the expected slowdown would be short-lived. The upturn could be anticipated within two years. I had cited the prior recession in 2000 as the likely scenario for the duration of 2008 slowdown. Hugh and I advised the builders not to get overly concerned.

We were wrong. Hugh and I had totally underestimated the suddenness and seriousness of what was about to come. Unemployment that was hovering at a stable 4.9%, when the year began, rose to over 7.3% by the end of the year. By November of the following year, the national unemployment rate had risen to 10.0%. In Henry County unemployment reached 10.4%.[15] If one calculated the numbers that were "under-employed", (those who were now taking menial jobs to survive), that number was closer to 20%. It was a rude awaking for some and a period of desperation for others.

Unable to find work and loaded with debt, many sought debt reliefs by filing bankruptcy. In Georgia one in every 60 households was now filing for bankruptcy protection. Henry County led the State with one in every 44 households. A trend that continued for several years as Henry County was number 5 in the nation for bankruptcies as late as 2016.[16] Many borrowers filed for bankruptcy protection to delay the repossession of their vehicles or foreclosure of their homes.

Foreclosures were now commonplace. Georgia was one of the leading states in the nation with Henry County out pacing the other counties on a per capita basis. In Georgia a lender could begin a foreclosure action on any delinquent real estate loan without a judicial hearing unlike in most states. It required only a foreclosure notice to the borrower and a four-week advertisement in the local paper. Properties would be auctioned off on the Henry County Courthouse steps the first Tuesday of every month between 10:00 am and 4:00 pm. Some Tuesdays there was such a crowd awaiting the sale to begin that one could hardly find a place to stand. Not every property that was being advertised would end in a foreclosure sale as some borrowers were able to "cure their defaults" (settle with the lender). But, in the end many of these delinquent borrowers lost their homes.

Today, I find myself reading the obituary columns. In those days I read the legal section of the *Henry Herald*, the county organ, as it was called. There were typically 35 to 40 pages of foreclosure notices. In April 2008 alone, Henry County had 412 foreclosure ads. That same month the Atlanta Metro area papers advertised approximately 7,000 properties for auction.

A significant event occurred on September 15, 2008, when Lehman Brothers filed for bankruptcy. [17] Its demise triggered what would be referred to as the "Great Recession". If one had polled everyone in the local McDonald's restaurant, 85% would admit that they had never heard of the Lehman Brothers. The other 15% would ask if they still lived in Ola.

Henry Lehman, a German immigrant living in Montgomery, Alabama, of all places, founded Lehman Brothers in 1850. It became the fourth largest U.S. investment bank with 25,000 employees. The bank made a colossal mistake when it purchased five mortgage lenders in 2003 and 2004. It aggressively securitized (underwritten) subprime mortgage loans in the billions of dollars...many of which later defaulted and resulted in huge losses for Lehman. Unaware of the seismic global impact of Lehman's collapse, the U.S. government failed to come to its rescue. History will show that the government erred in failing to bail out Lehman.

The bankruptcy of Lehman sent tremors through Wall Street. In September the stock market began its decline. The DOW average, which had peaked in October 2007 at 14,164, fell 778 points by September 28, 2008. By March 5, 2009, the DOW hit bottom at 6,594.[18] During this period, retirement accounts such as 401-ks and IRAs lost approximately 50% of their value.

The economic engine of Henry County was the "growth business". Fueled by the demand for housing, the local economy thrived. But nationally, as debt-burdened borrowers began to experience credit problems, mortgage delinquencies increased 50% by the end of 2008. As the problem loans mounted, the agencies that were guaranteeing these mortgages began to tighten the borrowing requirements. Only the strongest applicants were able to qualify for a mortgage. In essence, home sales to the average buyer came to a halt. Henry County now had a glut of unsold lots and houses. From my Econ 101 class, I witnessed first-hand the classic economic theory, "When supply out paces demand, prices will fall".[19] With few sales, the real estate market was at the threshold of a collapse, and home values began their precipitous decline.

Enterprise had significant growth in 2008 as it reached $95 million assets, approximately $79 million in loans, $84 million in deposits, and nearly $11 million in capital. It, however, incurred its first operating loss of $393,659. Henry County was not immune to the financial stresses that were being felt nationwide. Enterprise too felt the pain.

By the end of 2008, I admit that I was now getting concerned about the performance of the Bank. It was hard being an optimist when so many of Enterprise's respected customers were experiencing financial stress. The Bank, however, was determined to protect the employment of as many of its loyal staff as possible even while other banks were laying off.

Enterprise did its best to assist many individuals and small business owners during this period. I recall the various farm loans that were made in South Georgia. The Bank financed the construction of a veterinary clinic in Locust Grove, classrooms and a football facility for two private schools, numerous construction loans, and refinanced two daycare centers.

Although the Loan Officers were now making many quality loans, Enterprise had made too many large speculative real estate loans already on the books. As a result, in September the Banking Department cited the Bank in its next examination report as having a high concentration of commercial real estate loans (CREs). At the November meeting, the Board Members signed a M.O.U. (Memorandum of Understanding) with the Department of Banking. A M.O.U. was a commitment from Management and the Board to take certain corrective action to mitigate the cited weaknesses.

By the end of 2008, it was apparent that the Management needed to shift its focus from loan originations to capital preservation. Under the M.O.U. the Bank no longer needed loan originators. The Board reluctantly severed ties with Commercial Loan Officer, Karen Cooper. Commercial Loan Officer, David Stringer's services was terminated in December. David was an accountant and had been the former CEO of Founders Bank in McDonough now a BB&T branch. With these terminations, Enterprise lost the services of two talented lenders. The Board did approve the hiring of Jessica Richards to replace departing Sandi Roberts as Operations Officer. Later, Toni Turner, Leslie Waites, and Brenda Brown joined the bank.

Each bank was required to submit quarterly financial information

to the FDIC referred to as the CALL report. In my early banking days,
I prepared the five-page report manually. Our Call Report was now prepared by the Bank's CFO, electronically submitted, and contained more
than fifty pages. Since the data was readily available, the news media
used the information to report the financial conditions of the banks. In
June 2008 one such news item listed 185 Georgia banks that were considered to be "troubled banks".[20] Several banks doing business in Henry
County made the list. Enterprise had not.

An abbreviated summary of Enterprise Banking Company, Inc.'s
financial reports reflected the change of fortune at Enterprise. The profits enjoyed from rapid growth in 2007 gave way to an operating loss

Enterprise Financial Statement
2007 - 2008

	2007 ($)	2008 ($)
Total Loans	47,341,905	79,026.652
Loan Loss Reserve	625,301	914,516
Securities & Fed Funds	9,151,252	11,290,563
Fixed Assets	3,224,140	3,101,212
Total Assets	61,755,796	96,213,356
Total Deposits	50,090,896	80,350,016
Total Capital	11,085,133	11,364,810
Interest Income	3,609,104	4,650,325
Securities Income	353,848	184,588
Loans & Fees Charges	111,212	209,016
Interest Expenses	2,058,817	2,559,015
Personal Expenses	991,465	1,065,809
Administration	607,371	822,798
Contributions Loan Res	234,060	851,865
Net Income (Loss)	421,984	(256,284)

in 2008. The impact of the write down of local real estate loans was becoming more frequent. The real estate meltdown was underway. The Enterprise business plan that focused on reliable real estate lending was now an imperfect strategy.[21]

Changes were on the horizon.

CHAPTER SIX
CAUSES & UNINTENDED CONSEQUENCES

The older one becomes, the more one reminisces about the past and tries not to worry about the future. For me history had always been a favorite subject. In order to understand the plights of community banks like Enterprise, one must delve into the recent history of banking. External forces altered the dynamics of community banking and set the course for Enterprise. Economic recessions and booms are natural phenomenons, but economic crashes are man-made...usually contrived by those at the nation's capital. The leaders in Washington created a different banking landscape from the one to which I was familiar. The Great Recession was caused by the culmination of laws and events that occurred over a period of time and resulted in an eventual economic crash in late 2008. The outcome led to unprecedented financial distress for the banks.

From my office in McDonough, it was difficult to foresee how the subtle changes in Washington and at the State Capitol could impact a small bank in Henry County. The blame should go to well-meaning but bad government policies that contributed in steering the economy into an abyss. The outcomes were the "Housing Crash" → the "Credit Crunch" →the "Mortgage Crisis". As Hugh Morton had referred to in his book, *The Great American Housing Fiasco*, the "Mortgage Crisis" was the catalyst for bringing about the Great Recession.

Competition

The damage to community banks began with "bank deregulation". Principally, community banks like Enterprise were established to promote local commerce. Banks would provide a safe place to deposit money that could be loaned to meet the community's financial needs. The community in turn would see enhanced economic growth. Banks provided checking, savings, and loans to their customers. Their roles were clearly defined. The community banks knew their customers and were successful in this endeavor.

Large banks saw themselves as a broader financial service provider. In addition to the basic banking functions, these banks wanted to expand their services to include the securities business. Prior to the Great Depression, the banks were heavily involved in the stock market. As a result of the stock market crash in 1929 and the subsequent failure of many banks, Congress passed the Glass-Steagall Act. The legislation restricted banks from partaking in the securities business and established lending margins for stock loans. In essence, only brokerage firms were then allowed to trade in securities.

In November 1999, Congress repealed the Glass-Steagall Act and allowed the banks to reenter the securities business. Senator Phil Gramm, with the aid of a $300 million lobbying effort by the banking and financial-services industries, successfully spearheaded the bill through Congress. The Gramm-Leach Act opened the door to high returns that could be obtained only through high leverage and big risk-taking.[22] The Act not only deregulated financial institutions but brokerage firms and insurance companies as well. Everyone was now in the banking service business. To the community banks, it added a host of new competitors.

Initially, the large banks benefited greatly from their profitable security trading opportunities. But, as history repeated itself, many banks later experienced huge losses by having delved too deeply into various speculative investment products. The result was a host of new regulations for all banks. Many would be a burden on the smaller community banks.

Before 1996, Georgia banking laws prohibited banks from opening branches across county lines. There was a general belief that local communities were better served by local banks than by the large city banks. Under protectionism, local banks did not have to contend with out of town bank competition.[23] Georgia law had allowed every county to be granted a state charter for an independent community bank. With 159 counties, Georgia had an inordinate number of banks even with the absence of banks in the mostly rural counties.

New community banks were generally organized by local citizens and businessmen with the capital infusion coming from local shareholders. I recall the conversation with Joe Brannen, President of the Georgia Bankers Association. He was seeking my support of the proposed Georgia Statewide Branching bill. I was reluctant to endorse the change, because I was certain that it would bring a flood of outside banks to our market area.

Lawmakers passed the bill allowing statewide branching to begin in July 1998. Georgia quickly became a leader in the number of banks. Georgia's total exceeded all but five other states...more than New York and California, the most populated states. Many of the new banks were called de nova banks. A de nova bank was a newly chartered Georgia bank that was restricted from changing ownership in its first five years, later reduced to three years. Any newly organized bank had to receive approval from the regulatory agencies. Conditions of approval required community need and sufficient business to support the new bank. Consequently, most new banks chose to locate in high growth areas.

For a community, a new bank could be a source of readily available money. At that time a large portion of these funds would be used to fuel massive suburban real estate growth. Henry County was considered a prime location for lending opportunities for the new area banks. When I began my banking career, there were only four banks in Henry County.

By the end of 2007, the number had exponentially increased. The aggressive real estate lending by these local and neighboring banks created an overabundance of house and lot inventories.

In retrospect, the proliferation of new bank offices was not beneficial to all Georgia community banks. The unintended consequences were the loss of competitive advantage, subsequent reduction of profits, and decline in the community bank's franchise value.

The emergence of credit unions (CU) also added to the competitive fray. Credit unions differ from banks in that they are not-for-profit financial cooperatives that are owned by their members not shareholders. Credit unions' board of directors serve as unpaid volunteers that are elected by members.[24] Originally, credit unions had restrictive powers. Its customers had to be members of a particular homogeneous group. Today, anyone who had ever been on a Delta flight could open an account at Delta Credit Union. Seen as an aid to company employees and with their unique structure, Congress exempted CUs from federal income taxes. Once legislators broadened the powers of credit unions, they were allowed to offer services that once were limited just to banks. Credit unions inherited a legislated competitive advantage over the community banks.

Certainly, one can make an argument for the importance of credit unions as they provide consumer financial services that had become more difficult to obtain from the larger banks by individuals of modest means. Their popularity had increased to where approximately 43% of all account holders nationwide were members of a credit union. At of the end of 2016, there were 177 state and federally chartered credit unions operating in Georgia compared to 229 state and federally chartered banks.[25] In 2017 there were 5,844 credit unions nationwide.[26] Banks still have the bulk of the deposit market share; however, credit unions were continuing to make inroads in taking business away from community banks.

The credit union lobbyists contend that taxing credit unions would be a tax hike on the American consumers. Banks continue to be profitable. But, one must ask the question. Why should community banks subsidize credit unions? A $100 million community bank that earns 1% of its assets will pay annually from $300 to $360 thousand in income taxes. Shareholders will also pay income taxes on their dividends. Credit unions could provide cheaper financial services than banks, because they lacked the burden of income taxes.

As Clark Howard, an Atlanta syndicated talk-radio host and consumer advocate, said, "Credit unions are king and switching to a credit union can be the best move." A recent report from the American Customer Satisfaction Index took a look at the financial sector. Credit unions earned an 85, the highest score of any industry they researched. Bank of America, by contrast, got a 69. Small local community banks earned a very respectable 83.[27] The public perception of the community banks was closely aligned with credit unions when it came to customer satisfaction and service. Banks had an advantage in the services they provided to commercial customers. But without a strong commercial base, a community bank would have difficulty maintaining market share and profitability when going head-to-head against a credit union.

The functions of credit unions have drifted far from their intended mission as some have evolved into multi-billion-dollar institutions. The credit unions' tax exemption has cost Americans an estimated $24 billion in lost federal income taxes since 2004. According to Office of Management and Budget, the taxpayer cost will be another $25.4 billion over the next ten years. This ranks among the largest corporate tax loopholes. As the country's deficits have increased, the government can no longer afford a tax exemption that is not effective and whose purpose can no longer be justified.[28]

In 2008 the U.S. national debt was $8 trillion with an annual interest cost to the Treasury of $353 billion. The debt is estimated to reach $20.1 trillion by 2020 costing the taxpayers $474 billion annually. This expense will represent 9.7% of the national budget.[29] ...a frightening scenario. That being the case, what is the logic in allowing the number of tax-paying community banks to decline and having them replaced by tax exempt credit unions?

Laws and Regulations

After the Enron and WorldCom failures, Congress passed the Sarbanes Oxley Act in 2002. The new legislation was designed to encourage more responsibility and accountability by auditors, officers, and directors of public companies. In so doing, the auditing process became much more arduous and time consuming. All banks were now required to have on staff a Chief Financial Officer, who was a CPA. Since banks already had their own internal auditors and were examined regularly, the Sarbanes Oxley Act was an unnecessary regulatory burden for all banks. According to David Gill, President of The First State Bank, "Sarbanes Oxley requirements increased his bank's annual operating costs by $100,000."

Regulators decided banks should now adhere to an existing provision of GAAP (General Accepted Accounting Principles). With the adoption of "Mark to Market" accounting rules, a bank would now have to adjust the value of certain loans to a market value basis rather than carry them at their face value.[30] Unrealized losses from weak loans were to be recognized even if the borrowers were not in default. Under "Mark to Market" rules, the bank was expected to recognize a monetary loss before any loss occurred.

"Cost accounting" treatment of assets and liabilities that had been the standard during my entire banking career ended in 2008. "Mark to Market" became the norm. During a period of declining real estate values, "Mark to Market" accounting treatment of loans mercilessly eroded bank capital. At the end of the day, **"Mark to Market" rules destroyed Enterprise.**

Initially, all banks were assessed on equal terms by the FDIC for insuring its deposits. The practice continued until 1993. Banks were then assessed based on their risk rather than on a fixed rate for all banks.[31] Banks with inadequate capital and/or above average troubled loans would be expected to pay a higher fee. A calculation based on a percentage of a bank's average deposits during the previous quarter would increase correspondingly with the degree of regulatory criticism.

In 2009 Enterprise's FDIC annual fee assessment was approximately $400,000. The fee calculation was based on a percentage of deposits. The percentage more than tripled from the percentage calculated in 2005. The enormous fee, that followed, was the penalty for having a weak examination report. Like other banks in the area, those that could least afford to pay a fee were required to pay the most. According to David Gill, First State's annual fee had increased to approximately $2,100,000 for that same period.

Insurance companies commonly price premiums based on the level of risk. Those that are the highest risk pay the highest premiums. The logic makes sense as the riskiest coverages have the highest number of claims. Considering that the Deposit Insurance Fund is funded by the banks, this assumption gets somewhat skewed. Once a bank fails, the surviving banks are forced to cover the losses through increased premiums. The cost of liquidating a failed bank, in most cases, was greater than the cost of nursing such a troubled bank back to health. The assessment of extraordinary high fees to troubled banks only pushed them closer to failure. During times of stress, assessment of fees should have been deferred or reduced rather than increased. It seems very counterintuitive to strangle banks with such costs and further drain their capital resources. A moderation of the fee would have made more sense.

Housing and Mortgages

The inordinate demand for housing came about as legislators decided that the Federal government should take a more active role in ensuring that every American owned a home. Following the Great Depression, Franklin Roosevelt's New Deal initiative led Congress to establish the National Mortgage Association to provide local banks with federal money to fund home mortgages. Other government-sponsored agencies including Federal National Mortgage Association (FNMA), commonly known as Fannie Mae, and Federal Home Loan Mortgage Corporation (FHLMC), better known as Freddie Mac, evolved. Ginnie Mae, which remained a government organization, backed FHA-insured mortgages as well as Veterans Administration (VA) and Farmers Home Administration (FmHA) insured mortgages. These agencies guaranteed mortgages whereby lenders could sell the mortgages to investors, thus allowing lenders to relend their funds and expand the availability of mortgages.[32]

In 1999, the agencies came under pressure to expand mortgage loans to low and moderate-income borrowers.[33] The enforcement to banks came through the Community Reinvestment Act (CRA). The CRA mandated banks to make a certain number of loans to marginal borrowers in declining neighborhoods. It was a noble idea, but flawed. The lowered borrowing standards and relaxed underwriting requirements had undesired consequences.

The profitability of the mortgage business became so lucrative that proper underwriting was being ignored. A traditional banker would not have condoned such practices. But with a commission-driven mentality, the desire for profits outweighed sound lending.

In the early 2000s, unregulated investment banks began issuing

Mortgage Backed Securities (MBS) that contained pools of uninsured high-risk mortgage loans. Borrowers were approved with limited qualifications requiring no money down, no credit check, and/or no income verification. These loans became known as Subprime Mortgages and had a high default rate.

There were many abuses by those in the mortgage business...none greater than by a company with which Enterprise had a short-term business relationship. Taylor, Bean, & Whitaker (Taylor) had solicited mortgage loans from Enterprise to add to its mortgage pools. Taylor closed $35 billion in residential mortgage loans in 2007. At the time, it was the fifth-largest issuer of Ginnie Mae securities and by 2009 was servicing more than 500,000 mortgages including $51.2 billion Freddie Mac loans.

When Taylor was unable to cover overdrafts at Colonial Bank, it pledged $1 billion in mortgages, it did not own, to cover the $100 million-dollar overdraft. Taylor had already leveraged the mortgages as collateral for "Commercial Paper" debt. These collateralized debt obligations were issued and sold to raise cash. On August 4, 2009, the Federal Housing Administration (FHA) suspended the company from issuing any more FHA mortgage loans and Ginnie Mae mortgage-backed securities. Once under investigation, Taylor ceased business operations and terminated all of its approximately 2,000 employees at its Ocala, Florida, headquarters. Colonial Bank's regulator then seized the bank and appointed the FDIC as a receiver. Taylor later filed for bankruptcy protection. As a result, both companies were brought down by fraud involving individuals at Colonial Bank and Taylor, Bean, & Whitaker. Their shenanigans added fuel to the worsening mortgage crisis. Later, six individuals including Lee Farkas, the majority owner of Taylor, pleaded guilty for their roles in the fraudulent scheme.

My first cousin Josef Ackermann was the CEO of Deutsche Bank at the time of his bank's purchase of the worthless "Commercial Paper". His parents and my parents were married in a joint wedding ceremony in Zürich. Ironically, Joe and I both became bankers, but at different ends of the spectrum…one, CEO of one of the largest banks in the world and the other CEO of one of the smallest banks. Enterprise was not affected by all of the wrongdoings by the executives of Taylor, Bean, & Whitaker. After the litigation, Deutsche Bank, however, suffered a sizable loss.[34]

Rhonda Foster's responsibility as Enterprise's Mortgage Loan Officer was to originate mortgage loans. At the peak she processed 5 to 10 applications a month for individuals wishing to buy an existing home or to purchase a new spec home from one of the Bank's builder customers. Since it was not possible for a small bank to fund 30-year fixed rate loans, she took the application, verified the information, obtained the support documents, and passed the loan package to an upstream mortgage lender. The mortgage lender had the loan underwritten by FHA, VA, or one of the other Federal Mortgage Agencies. With a Federal guarantee, the mortgage lender added the loan to a mortgage package and sold it to a large investor. For this service, Enterprise received an origination fee. Enterprise was not required to fund the loans nor was it exposed to any future risk if the borrowers did not pay.

Rhonda did not waste her time with loans where she determined the borrower had underwriting issues such as questionable credit or insufficient income. I can say with some level of confidence that Enterprise originated very few subprime loans. So, it is hard to comprehend the sheer numbers of these loans that were being originated by lenders in Henry County and nationwide at that time.

Mortgage-backed securities have been around for a while. When purchasing these securities for the Bank, the underlying mortgages were fully guaranteed by government agencies and/or covered by PMI insurance.[35] Private Mortgage Insurance, referred to as PMI, was a type of mortgage insurance that protected the lender if the borrower did not pay. These securities had a AAA rating, were considered to be safe investments, and offered a higher yield to investors than U.S. Treasuries. This changed as some mortgage lenders added non-guaranteed and/or subprime mortgages to mortgage pools. These pools of loans were then sold to unsuspecting investors.

The most popular mortgage product at the time was the non-qualifying adjustable rate loan. These loans had an initial low interest rate called a "teaser rate". When the interest rate reset to the new adjusted rate, the mortgage payment amount could correspondingly increase significantly. The marginal borrower now could no longer afford his home. For that reason, many of these mortgages went into default. The purchasers of the mortgages would then have to rely on the sale of the foreclosed real estate to recoup their investment. Many of these mortgage pools that were thought to be AAA investments were in actuality "junk bonds". All the while, senior bank management and the bond traders were receiving enormous bonuses from the profits generated by these trades.

The perception that a home would always be a safe investment was no longer the rule. No one foresaw the number of delinquencies and foreclosures that soon followed. The credit crunch ensued and the real estate bubble burst shortly thereafter. The real estate market collapsed. The Atlanta metro area including Henry County was one of the hardest hit regions in the U.S.

The regulators had been overwhelmed in the early 1980s by the crisis that plagued the banks in the oil producing states and the Savings and Loan financial institutions, (S & Ls), nationwide. This time around, the regulators were determined to head off another such occurrence. Unfortunately, the regulators were late in reacting to the real estate problems. The harsh demands they imposed on the banks created many unintended consequences. Remedying the problem through more regulations was not the answer. Yet, regulators were relentless in the pressure exerted on banks through their mandates.

·························· Profits ··························

One of the duties of the Federal Reserve Bank was to maintain the stability of the nation's economy. The Fed accomplished this through its monetary policies. One of its methods was the control of interest rates. The Federal Funds Rate was the rate of interest that banks charged or paid one another when borrowing or lending money overnight. For longer borrowing periods, the Discount Rate was the interest rate paid by a bank when borrowing directly from the Fed. These rates impacted the cost of deposits and the yields received from loans and securities. By the end of 2008, the Fed Funds rate had declined to one-quarter of one per-cent (0.025%) from 4.25% a year earlier. Enterprise was allocating 75% of its deposits to loans and remaining 25% was being invested in low risk securities. The significance of the precipitous drop in rates meant that Enterprise would realize a lower return from it excess deposits. The Bank was now dependent exclusively on lending for its revenue at a time when the lending risks were at their highest.

During a discussion about the direction of banking in 2008, a com-ment that resonated with me came from a senior banking department official. His greatest concern was that banks were ceasing to be profit-able. With the increased competition, the additional regulations, and the changing economy, he did not see how new banks could generate earn-ings. I did not buy his story then, but I soon learned that he was correct.

These external forces, whether by design or not, drastically reduced the number of Georgia banks. During my first 30 years in banking there were so very few Georgia bank failures that I could not recall more than a handful. It was now the thinking of some in Washington that the banking public could be better served by a vast network of mega banks than by individual community banks. The "Mom and Pop" business model was giving way to the Walmarts of the world. In 1985 there were 18,033 FDIC insured banks in the U.S. That number declined to 7,658 by 2010.[36] The majority of the decline was in the number of smaller community banks.

As per Hugh Morton's book, *The Great American Housing Fiasco*, Henry County was a victim of urban sprawl. There was an abundance of money, accessibility into the building and developing businesses, and the attraction of potential profit. The rural setting began to fill with "pipe farms" (named for the vertical PVC pipes that marked the locations of the underground utilities) that became the next residential subdivision. Henry County soon was saturated with lots and houses. Whether starter homes or homes in upper-scale subdivisions, residents from neighboring northern counties were choosing to relocate to Henry. These newcomers were motivated by the improving school system, the rural setting, and the convenience of I-75 and I-675. Mesmerized by the lure of profits, that it would bring, the bankers embraced the building boom.

Enterprise also got caught in the idealistic trap. The builders and bankers could do no wrong. The demand for housing raised home values by 41.2% from 2000 to 2006. Home prices, however, peaked in 2006. The market correction followed with a 45.1% decline in values from 2006 to 2011.[37]

Enterprise had now gained momentum as it had booked $47 million in loans in 2006 and 2007. The loan portfolio surpassed $79 million by the end of 2008. The Bank's Lending Policy did have some built-in protection to offset possible declines in the real estate values. Amortizing real estate loans were limited to 80% or less of the appraised of value, single pay loans were capped at 75%, and unimproved real estate (raw land) could not exceed 65%. Even with these prudent collateral margins, most real estate loans originated from 2006 to 2008 were all underwater by 2010.

Enterprise's meltdown cannot be attributed to one particular event, but to a chain reaction of all the aforementioned causes and effects.

It had been a long wild ride…a party for many. As the builders, developers, real estate agents, and bankers were celebrating their successes, boasting about the money they had made, and anticipating the next "can't miss" real estate deal, the party came to an end, and the lights went out. In the darkness there was much turmoil and confusion. In the days that followed, the party goers found themselves with financial hangovers and empty wallets. Everyone wondered how this could have happened!

CHAPTER SEVEN

2009 THE YEAR OF SURVIVAL

2009 began with great trepidation. In late 2008, NetBank and Integrity Bank of Alpharetta were the first two Georgia banks of the period that could not meet the regulatory capital requirements and were closed. FDIC was named the Receiver. Later, Washington Mutual, one of the nation's largest mortgage lenders, was closed including their offices in Henry County.

The possibility of a major economic crisis facing our nation that could take down the banks was becoming more probable. The Fed was getting concerned about the evaporation of capital in its banks. The large banks, which were considered to be "too big to fail", began to shore up their capital. They could easily sell additional shares of stock to increase their capital bases. There were plenty of willing investors that perceived the big bank stocks to be cheap. Bank stock prices had declined substantially from their record highs. I owned a small amount of Bank of America stock that my brother-in-law, Kirk Scruggs, had given me while he worked for C & S Bank in Atlanta. I had added shares through its dividend investment plan where I had paid as much as $54 per share. The stock was now trading for around $4 a share. Bank of America through its various mergers and acquisitions, including Atlanta's C & S Bank, had become the largest U.S. bank.

On the other hand, with their long-term survival in question, smaller community banks had little hope of finding investors. Most community banks were experiencing declining and/or non-existent earnings.

Dividends were being suspended. Banks were cutting back and laying off staff.

With the blessing of Congress, the Fed established a plan to provide a means for banks to have access to capital. The Troubled Asset Relief Program (TARP) was a multi-faceted program sponsored by the United States government. It was designed to purchase bad loans from financial institutions and/or to provide them with a vehicle to strengthen their equity. The $700 billion plan was signed into law by President Bush on October 3, 2008.[38] It was the Board's hope that the Treasury could make funds available to Enterprise via the TARP program. The 30-page contractual agreement was in essence a five-year loan commitment. Enterprise would only be required to pay interest initially but would be required to repay the entire sum in 5 years. The Fed reasoned that the local economy would improve during the five-year period to the degree whereby Enterprise would be able to repay its obligation.

Management applied for $4 million in TARP money. To its disappointment Enterprise, along with every other community bank in Henry County, had their applications denied. The only banks awarded the TARP funds were those that appeared not to need assistance. The smaller community banks, were now in desperate need of a helping hand, but the Fed and Congress ignored their pleas for assistance.

Across Highway 20 from Enterprise was a Wachovia branch. As one of the more venerable banks in the U.S., it began its operation in Winston-Salem, N.C. in 1879. Wachovia expanded into 21 states with 3,300 offices nationally and 40 international offices. It was a very successful bank until it increased its concentration of mortgage loans with the purchase of Golden West Financial in California. Wachovia eventually crumbled under the weight of the bad mortgage loans it inherited in the deal. With Wachovia in trouble, Federal regulators interceded and forced a merger between it and Wells Fargo in late 2008.[39] Upon learning of the news, I commented at the next regular staff meeting, "If Wachovia could not survive, what chance would a small bank such as Enterprise have?"

The parade of local bank failures continued with the closing of FirstBank Financial Services located down the street on Hwy 20 in February 2009 and FirstCity Bank in Stockbridge in March. FirstBank Financial Services, originally named First Bank of Henry County, was managed by Randy Dixon, President, who was my former commercial loan officer at First State. Randy had died of cancer prior to the closing of his bank.

FirstCity Bank was located in Stockbridge and was managed by Mark Conner, its President. Mark was a former real estate agent and handled the marketing for the Eagles Landing's development. I recall having lunch with Mark to work out a line of credit for his boss, J. T. Williams and Killearn Properties, the owners of Eagles Landing.

Later in May 2009, the closing of Silverton Bank, formally The Bankers Bank, had a devastating impact on Enterprise and all the community banks in Georgia. Silverton was Enterprise's chief corresponding bank. As the correspondent bank, Silverton provided services that a small bank could not handle on its own. These included check clearing, purchase and sale of investment securities, credit card programs, insurance programs, etc. More importantly, Silverton could assist in the funding of our larger business loan requests by facilitating the sale of portions of the loan to other banks. Loan participations would allow Enterprise to spread the loan risk and stay within its legal lending limits. Silverton's shareholders were the individual community banks, and the CEO's from these banks oversaw its operation. In such a relationship, Enterprise, as a small bank, was able to be competitive with the larger banks in the area. The service support and available line of credit that were crucial to Enterprise were taken away.[40]

I was elected to serve on The Bankers Bank (TBB) Board in 1996. A banker from each of the 10 congressional districts made up the original Board of Directors. The Board in its oversight approved the appointment of senior officers and reviewed and approved the larger loans. I had the privilege of serving on the Board for five years and acted as Chairman in 2000.

Shortly after I resigned from the TBB Board in 2001, Bruce Leonard, its long-term CEO, left the TBB in 2003. I had a great working

....

THE ATLANTA JOURNAL-CONSTITUTION August 28, 2011

Silverton's rapid rise and fall

Money no object when it came to its growth. The effects of its failure on partner lenders is detailed in lawsuits.

By Russell Grantham

By 2008, Silverton Bank's lavish annual soirées at Ritz-Carlton's Amelia Island resort were the place to be each summer for Atlanta institutions' rapidly growing crowd of customers – hundreds of community bankers from across the nation. The bankers heard hard-sell pitches on why they should become partners in Silverton's rapid rise to become the nation's largest so-called "bankers bank".

But it turned out that Atlanta based Silverton was on an express trip that ended in oblivion . The fallout from its failure in May 2009-Georgia's largest bank failure ever-helped sink dozens of its customer banks as well.

Silverton's failure "present a textbook example of officers and directors being asleep at the wheel and robotically voting" to approve risky loans and "expansive and extravagant spending"- even as the real estate and financial markets were rapidly deteriorating in 2007 and 2008, the Federal Deposit Insurance Corp. said in a lawsuit filed last week in U.S. District Court in Atlanta.

Silverton was not a typical bank. It didn't do business with the public. Instead, it was a "correspondent bank" that handled both routine and complex services for its 1,400 member banks.

As the economy and Silverton's finances were wilting in 2007 and 2008, the agency alleges, the bank continued expanding, hiring employees and taking on hundreds of millions of dollars of risky real estate loans. During this

78

Silverton's rapid rise and fall *(cont.)*

period it built a swank new $35 million headquarters in Buckhead and grew to 400 employees. It paid almost $4.9 for two executive aircraft-one sold to Silverton by its CEO-bringing its fleet to three.

Then it spent $3.8 million more constructing a new aircraft hangar, and millions more on a staff of eight pilots and meetings with investors and customers at a resort at Sea Island, Ga. and Amelia Island, Fla.

To fund its operations Silverton depended on members banks' cash deposits in their check clearing accounts and short-term investment. For each member those accounts often totaled millions of dollars – well above the FDIC's deposit guarantee of $250,000.

....

relationship with Bruce. I felt that he had provided the bank with the needed leadership to transform the TBB to an effective correspondent bank in Georgia and adjacent states. Tom Bryan, who had been the bank's Executive Vice President and former Senior Investment Officer, assumed the CEO role. Under his administration, the bank raised the bar and set its sight on becoming the largest corresponding bank in the nation. There were 17 such banks at the time with 15 remaining today.[41] TBB was granted the transfer of regulatory control from the Georgia Department of Banking to the Comptroller of Currency. The national bank affiliation allowed its operations to expand outside of Georgia. In so doing, the Board elected to change its name from The Bankers Bank to Silverton Bank (Silverton). Silverton eventually served more than 1,500 community banks nationwide. At the time of its failure, Silverton had $4.1 billion in total assets and $3.1 billion in total deposits. The Silverton's failure was the largest failure of a bank headquartered in Georgia.

One of the most appreciated services that Silverton provided to client banks was loan participations. Rural area banks, that had excess deposits, but little loan demand, were always looking to the growth area banks for loans. The loan participations with other banks would bolster the rural bank's bottom line. Silverton acted as the facilitator of these transactions. Silverton found that originating loans and selling participations to be more profitable than just providing correspondent bank services. One particular participation loan that the Enterprise Board was asked to consider was the Merrill Ranch Loan, a $100 million loan secured by a multi-use development in Arizona. Silverton kept $7.5 million of the loan and sold the remaining loan amount to 60 downstream participating community banks. Many were small rural banks. Gordon Skeen, a member of Enterprise's Loan Committee, was familiar with the guarantors of the Merrill Ranch loan. He recalled the difficulty his former bank experienced in collecting payments. Thankfully, Gordon convinced the Board to decline the loan participation opportunity. The Merrill Ranch project eventually went belly up. Silverton, which had been a catalyst for community bank growth and success, now was instrumental in creating a significant loan problem for many of its member banks.

One of the casualties of the Merrill Ranch loan debacle was Peoples Bank headquartered in Winder. Chris Maddox, a former Chairman and interim CEO of Silverton and CEO of Peoples Bank, purchased a loan participation. Chris' father, Charles Maddox, was one of the founders of The Bankers Bank and its most respected and influential Board member. Tragically, the Merrill Ranch loan default further weaken the already struggling Peoples Bank. The bank was closed in September 2010.

I vividly remember the telephone call I received from another banker warning me of Silverton's eminent closing. Enterprise had a substantial amount on deposit in its clearing and overnight Federal Funds accounts. I was informed that these deposits would be insured only up to the $250,000 FDIC limit. If Silverton were to be closed by regulators, Enterprise would lose the majority of its cash reserve. Not willing to take the risk, I reluctantly transferred all of the Bank's deposits to the Texas Bankers Bank. I later learned that many other community banks had moved their accounts as well. The run on Silverton Bank that week had hastened its closing.

Silverton's rapid expansion costs and its aggressive lending activity led to its demise. The FDIC later brought a $71 million lawsuit against the Directors, the Chief Lending Officer, and the Chief Credit Officer.[42] The insurance carrier was left holding the bag. I had mixed emotions over the fact that my actions in transferring the deposits had contributed to Silverton's closing, but it had probably saved Enterprise.

Two banks that had ties to Henry County were closed in June of 2009. Southern Community Bank of Fayetteville opened in 2000 and had reached $415 million in assets before being taken over by United Community Bank of Blairsville.[43] Southern Community had a branch in Locust Grove. It's Chairman, Tom Reece, was one of Enterprises' largest commercial borrowers. The closing of his bank was a financial blow to Mr. Reece and led to the decline of his financial empire. The Bank was fortunate to lure its Chief Operating Officer, Jessica Richards, to join Enterprise and replace the departing Sandi Roberts.

The $221 million Neighborhood Community Bank of Newnan also founded in 2000 had a large loan presence in Henry County. Its failure was influenced in part by bad Henry County real estate loans. CharterBank of West Point assumed only its deposits.[44]

In December 2009 RockBridge Commercial Bank (RockBridge) in Atlanta with $294 million in assets was closed. RockBridge was launched in 2006 with a hefty $36 million in capital. It catered to small and mid-sized businesses and their banking needs. Its Board included the general counsel for Home Depot, Inc. and a former partner of Porter Keadle

Moore, a major Atlanta accounting firm.[45]

Ann Cross was a Commercial Loan Officer with The Bankers Bank and had accepted a similar position at RockBridge. While with The Bankers Bank, she had handled the bank director loans that were used to acquire Dorsey State Bank. In moving to RockBridge, she had solicited the refinance of several of these TBB stock loans including one of mine.

In the case of Silverton and RockBridge, no bank stepped forward to acquire the failing banks. As a result, the FDIC acted as Receiver and was responsible for the liquidation of its assets and liabilities. FDIC's greatest challenge was the management of the complicated loan portfolios.

CHAPTER EIGHT
A TOUGH TIME TO BE A BANKER

The regulatory agencies determined the "Safety and Soundness" of a bank through a grading system it called C.A.M.E.L.S. (Camels Rating). Like all government agencies, the FDIC used clever acronyms. The Camels rating was a standardized formula used in its examinations. The components of a bank's financial condition are assessed according to its: Capital Adequacy, Asset Quality, Management Capability, Earnings, Liquidity, and Sensitivity to Risk[46]. Ratings were given from 1 (being the best) to 5 (being the worst) in each of the above categories. The average of all the categories became the overall composite rating for the bank. The composite rating measured the financial strengths and weaknesses of a bank and the degree of risk it posed to the Deposit Insurance Fund.

At the September 2008 examination, the Department of Banking had downgraded Enterprise's Camels composite rating to a "3". During earlier years, my previous bank was examined at least annually. At these examinations it was rare not to receive some criticism. The on-sight examiners would always find some areas that they deemed needed improvement. A composite rating of "1" was very difficult to obtain. I was always satisfied with "2". With the "3" overall rating, the State regulator also issued Enterprise a M.O.U (Memorandum of Understanding). The Banking Department's chief concern was the deteriorating real estate loan portfolio, and its impact on the bank's Loan Loss Reserve and Capital. The Board considered the M.O.U. a serious matter and began addressing the problems cited in the M.O.U.

The downgrade was the beginning of a difficult period for Enterprise and a critical juncture in the Board's oversight of the Bank. Enterprise had plenty of liquidity as existing customers were continuing to roll over and/or purchase new C.D.s. Neither the Bank's customer base nor the banking public had lost confidence in the Bank. Enterprise's 2% C.D. interest rate offered at that time equaled the highest rate in Henry County. Given the difficult economic environment, the challenge was maintaining an adequate level of reserve and preserving capital.

It was a reality in the banking business that lending money had its inherent risk; thus, the importance of having the Loan Loss Reserve. The reserve was referred to by the regulators as ALLL, Allowance for Loan and Lease Losses. With the anticipation of certain loan losses, Enterprise made periodic contributions to a Loan Loss Reserve. Bank regulations provided guidelines as to how to determine the amount needed to keep in the reserve. Enterprise allocated, as a monthly expense, a portion of its earnings as a contribution to its reserve. When a loan was deemed non-collectable, its balance was charged to the loan reserve. In so doing, the loan loss would have already been accounted for and would not have resulted in a non-budgeted expense. During normal times, an amount of 1.0% to 2.0% of total outstanding loans was a sufficient reserve to offset charge offs.

One of the primary duties of Randy Smith, the CFO, was to calculate the monthly amount needed in the Loan Loss Reserve. He relied on the loan classifications provided by the Internal Auditor and/or the Loan Review Consultant. Each loan was evaluated, graded, and given a Pass, Special Mention, or an Adverse Classification. The rating was based in part by the payment performance, strength of the borrower, and value of the collateral. Adversely Classified Loans were divided into Substandard, Doubtful, or Loss. From the degree of risk, a percentage of the loan amount was set aside in the reserve: Pass and Special Mentioned Classified Loans required

0% to be reserved, Substandard Classified Loans required 10% to be reserved, Doubtful Classified Loans required 50% to be reserved, and Loans deemed to be a Loss required 100% to be reserved.[47] The compilation of all the classified loans and their corresponding percentages determined the aggregate balance needed to be held in the Loan Loss Reserve. The reserve balance was a forecast of future loan losses. Bank earnings were now insufficient to cover the increasing amount of anticipated loan losses. The contributions to the reserve negatively impacted Enterprise's capital and these operating losses had begun to cloud the Bank's future. Each additional loss reduced the Bank's capital.

By now most borrowers were cash poor and "under water" with their real estate holdings. "Under water" meant a borrower owed more on the real estate than it was worth. When the borrower's source of cash eroded and his paying ability became questionable, his loan was downgraded to Substandard or worse. If the loan deteriorated further and the borrower was unable to pay, the loan was further downgraded. At this point, the borrower and/or the Bank would have to rely on the sale of the collateral for repayment. At each stage of the grading process, Enterprise made the appropriate contributions to Loan Loss Reserve. As part of the process, Enterprise estimated a reasonable amount it could expect to receive from the sale of collateral less any anticipated carrying costs when repayment was in doubt. If the expected return was less than what was owed and the amount already reserved, the difference was written down and charged against the Loan Loss Reserve. Maintaining adequate Loan Loss Reserves was now also being undermined by the decline in real estate values.

In light of the M.O.U., the Board considered not lending altogether. This strategy would eliminate the risk of any new loans going bad and further draining the Loan Loss Reserve. Since earnings were still vital to the operation of the Bank and were relied upon to replenish Capital, the Board decided to continue lending. The focus was finding stronger borrowers and making better loans. The lending was directed to borrowers that had sufficient net worth and income to service their debt. The Bank was seeking borrowers that had the ability to pay without any dependency on the volatile real estate market. Enterprise shifted lending efforts from builders and developers to medical practitioners and business professionals. As to the existing borrowers with classified loans... the Board was confident, that even with their weakening financial positions, most borrowers could work out of their troubled real estate loans over time.

News about banks were now hot topics on television and in newspapers. The reporting of negative banking news became an everyday occurrence. Several business news services provided periodic updates of the status of troubled banks through a method which became known as the Texas Ratio. The ratio was developed by a banking analyst as a way to predict bank failures during the Texas' 1980s recession.[48] The ratio measured the relationship between the bank capital to its non-performing real estate loans. In March of 2009, Enterprise made the Texas Ratio list for the first time. Enterprise was ranked at 110th. There were 109 Georgia banks with more real estate loan problems as a percent of capital than Enterprise had.

In search of ways to strengthen Enterprise's capital position, the Board met with the Directors of Community Capital Bank in July 2009. The purpose of the meeting was to discuss the benefits of a merger. Community Capital was one of the few remaining community banks in Clayton County. The two banks were located in adjoining counties but competed in the same market areas. Each bank had only a small number of shareholders, and each had a Subchapter S tax designation. Both banks were operating under a similar business plan and had a concentration of real estate loans. There was a great deal of commonality between the banks including the number of troubled real estate loans. Suffering from the same ills, a merger would not have made sense. The combined capital would not have been sufficient to elevate the surviving bank to a "well capitalized" position required by the regulators.

In July 2009 the FDIC began its Safety and Sound audit of the Bank. The regulators appeared to be on a mission. The FDIC had reinforced the Atlanta Regional Office with additional examiners. From what Management was hearing and reading, the new examiners assigned to audit the metro area banks were portraying the role of old west "gunslingers". They were going to clean up the banks and run all the bad bankers out of town. It was the regulator's view point that the only way to resolve the banking crisis was to rid the country of its under-capitalized banks. FDIC was determined to head off another 1980 like crisis.

The current crisis presented a new set of challenges for the regulators. To Enterprise, the economic problems it was facing were of a different nature than those experienced by the S & Ls and the oil state banks of the 1980s. The failure of S & Ls was a result of a profit squeeze. S & Ls were funding long-term fixed mortgages with short-term savings accounts and rate sensitive C.D.s. A typical 30-year mortgage rate was 8.75% in the 1980s. The S & Ls had an adequate spread when its savings rate was fixed at 5%. Once Congress allowed deposit rates to fluctuate, C.D. rates slowly began to climb. As banks and S & Ls were allowed to offer new money-market accounts, some institutions were paying introductory rates of 16%. The cost of funds rose dramatically while at the same time, the mortgages were locked in at much lower rates. The outcome for these S & Ls was losses in income and erosion of liquidity.

The bank failures of the 1980s were concentrated in the oil producing areas primarily in Texas. The rapid rise in oil prices that followed the OPEC oil embargo created an economic boom in the area. Those in the oil business were getting rich. The money that flowed into the banks found its way to borrowers seeking to invest in the now lucrative real estate market.[49] When oil prices crashed in 1987, so did real estate values. The banks that had loaned too heavily in speculative commercial real estate struggled.

The 2008 recession affected banks predominately in the high growth areas of the U.S. Many parts of Georgia were suffering from over-development. Henry County had an abundance of residential lots and spec houses. The demand for new housing was now waning, and real estate prices were declining. The Board, nevertheless, assumed that the oversupply would eventually correct itself through the utilization of the inventory. Historically, there had always been a great demand for housing in the "sunshine states". Metro Atlanta and Henry County were no exception. The old adage that God was not making any more real estate gave credence to the fact that real estate values would always rise over the long haul. Patience not panic should have been the mindset. Closing hundreds of banks for having troubled loans seemed to be an over kill. Euthanizing the banks to control the ailing real estate market made little sense.

Not everyone supported the FDIC's treatment of banks. A bill introduced by U.S. Representative Lynn Westmoreland would require a congressional study of the banking crisis. Some of the areas that would be investigated, were the so-called "Loss Share Agreements" and the "mark to market" accounting practices. An article in the AJC quoted a finance professor from the University of North Carolina in Charlotte. "We have erred on the side of lax regulation and now we've erred on the side of over-regulation...community banks have been pecked to death."[50] The Director of the FDIC, Sheila Bair, discounted the wisdom of such efforts. She criticized certain members of Congress who had insisted that the FDIC ease up.

It was now the focus of the FDIC to gain regulatory control of the large money center banks. The first priority was to have the banks legitimize their balance sheets. Banks would be required to write down questionable assets. As the write downs mounted and eroded the bank's capital, the concern shifted to the health of the banks. The survival of large banks was considered critical in revitalizing the slumping economy. These banks were deemed "too big to be allowed to fail". On the other hand, there were many small community banks that had no national significance but were important to their local communities. These like Enterprise deserved additional time to resolve their problems.

....

THE ATLANTA JOURNAL-CONSTITUTION July 30, 2011

House passes bill to study rescue efforts

Measure introduced by Ga. representative calls practices into question

By: J. Scott Trubey

The U.S. House of Representatives approved late Thursday a bill from a Georgia congressman that would investigate if the government's efforts to clean up distressed and failed banks are doing more harm than good.

"Community banks are the economic engine of our towns and cities and the large number of failed banks in Georgia can have a devastating effect on our economic recovery," the Coweta County Republican said in a news release.

"Without these local lenders, job growth and economic investment can dry up – an unmistakable reality proven by the fact that the 10 states with highest number of failures also have some the highest unemployment and foreclosure rates in the country," Westmoreland said.

....

Local lawmakers were seeing their districts being decimated economically by the closing of the community banks. Butts, Henry, Fayette, Clayton, and Coweta Counties were severely impacted. Lynn Westmoreland, U.S. Representative, who resided in Grantville located in Coweta County, and David Scott, U.S. Representative for the 13th District of Georgia, representing portions of Clayton, Fayette, and Henry Counties questioned the aggressive stance of the regulators. Lynn Westmoreland and David Scott introduced a bill to investigate the government's efforts in how it was

treating the banks. The bill did not gain the support in the Senate. Therefore, the shrinking in the number of community banks continued.

....

THE ATLANTA JOURNAL-CONSTITUTION August 17, 2011
Regulators called too tough

Lawmakers say rules are hindering recovery.

By: J. Scott Trubey

Banking regulation might have been too lax before the housing bust, but federal law makers at a hearing in Newnan questioned Tuesday, whether the crackdown since then has unfairly punished community banks and slowed the industry's recovery.

Banks that are too big to fail survived. "Banks that are too small have been cut loose," said U.S. Rep. Lynn Westmoreland, a Republican from Coweta County who is also a former home builder.

More than a 100 people – mostly bankers, home builders or regulators – attended the hearing. Westmoreland was joined by three other members of a subcommittee of the House Financial Services Committee, including Rep. David Scott, a Democrat who represents areas of south and west metro Atlanta.

They said regulators from the Federal Deposit Insurance Corp., the Federal Reserve and Office of the Comptroller of the Currency may have become overzealous in the enforcement of community banks. Bankers, they said, complain of "mixed messages from regulators, especially when it comes to helping distressed borrowers.

Critics have alleged uneven treatment of troubled banks and said methods the government uses to dispose of failed banks harm borrowers and could be hindering the economic recovery by restricting credit.

Regulators, however, said their practices are designed to return the industry to health so that banks can help fund an economic rebound.

Westmoreland and Scott are co-sponsoring a bill to require the inspector general of the FDIC and the nonpartisan Government Accountability Office to examine enforcement practices and sales of failed banks to healthy rivals.

So-called loss-share deals are often offered to attract buyers of failed banks. Regulators say loss-share deals have saved the FDIC's deposit insurance fund, which backstops deposits, $40 billion. Critics charge the deals result in fire sales of assets and injure borrowers.

The bill also would examine certain accounting practices that critics say force banks to write down the value of certain performing loans, often involving real estate. "Most of the banks that failed in Georgia have been appraised out of business."

CHAPTER NINE
THE DREADED CONSENT ORDER

When one reads the Banking Department and FDIC regulations and procedures manuals, one will discover that these compare in length to *Gone with the Wind* or *War and Peace*, and are as interesting as reading a phone book. It is virtually impossible to digest or comprehend all the laws and regulations they contain. Although operating a bank within the regulatory parameters was nearly impossible, there was nevertheless no forgiveness for banks that deviated too far from policy or committed law violations. To those banks the regulatory agencies would most likely impose some type of corrective action. The most punitive action levied by the FDIC was the Consent Order.

The next examination at Enterprise occurred in the summer of 2009 and was conducted by the FDIC. Henry County was mired in the midst of a deep and far reaching recession. Enterprise's financial condition mirrored the economic struggles of its customers. So much of the Bank's loan portfolio were loans to those who depended on an active real estate market. Henry County was having a real estate meltdown. For the most part, borrowers were renewing their loans, albeit managing to pay only the interest. The examination was a disaster as the examiners found little not to criticize. Enterprise had not been able to satisfy all of the conditions that were set forth in the Georgia Department of Banking's M.O.U. which only gave the FDIC more ammunition to find weaknesses.

The most damaging and unexpected criticism was Enterprise's real estate loan appraisals. The examiners were now enforcing a recent Contravention Interagency Policy that required the periodic re-appraisal or re-evaluation of real estate collateral. The Bank was cited for not having current appraisals. The appraisals the Bank did obtain, the appraisers' methods used in determining values were questioned. The Bank had raw land and construction loans that were renewed without updated appraisals. The regulators deemed new appraisals necessary as real estate values were on the decline, whereby the banks were not accurately recognizing the subsequent loan impairments. The examiners also mentioned that some of the existing appraisals did not discount the values adequately to account for the longer holding periods and declining sales prices if foreclosed. Since most of these loans were renewed and were not past due, the Loan Officers had not obtained the second appraisals. The requirement seemed unnecessary and would be an additional expense to the struggling borrowers and/or the Bank.

The examiners reviewed the bulk of Enterprise's real estate loans, specifically the unimproved land, lot, and construction loans. They determined that some should be reclassified as substandard. By not having current or acceptable real estate appraisals, the examiners performed their own evaluations of the cited properties. Such a practice had not been a standard procedure in any previous examinations. The examiner used an evaluation approach that estimated the present value based on an arbitrary formula including the estimated future sales prices less the holding costs of the property. These calculations were very conservative, and in each case resulted in a significantly lower evaluation than the amount stated in the appraisal on file. The regulator-adjusted appraisals contradicted the valuations of the Certified Appraiser. The end result was the write down of several real estate loans. Comedian Steven Wright stated, that "42.7% of all statistics were made up on the spot". Enterprise considered some of the revised appraisal numbers to have followed the same logic.

Many of the cited borrowers had never been seriously delinquent, but their credit lines got adversely classified anyway. Very few of the borrowers who had construction or lot inventory loans were spared. Most borrowers with adversely classified loans at other lending institutions had their Enterprise loans downgraded. Many experts had surmised that the worst was over, and a real estate recovery was just around the corner. Hence, the aggressive write down of real estate loans was difficult to comprehend and a bitter pill to swallow.

Sadly, as a result of the examination, Enterprise was required to write off more than $3 million in addition to the $2 million it had already internally written off. Enterprise wrote off more loans on that infamous day than had been written off at my previous bank, First State, during my entire 25 years as CEO. It was quite a shock and difficult to rationalize the harsh regulator treatment toward Enterprise.

To emphasis the point... one loan that received a sizable write down was a large lot inventory loan. The Bank was well acquainted with the borrower and had refinanced his lots that were previously financed by another lender. From the initial appraisal, Enterprise had loaned 75% of the value of the lots. Since the borrower had also pledged $500,000 in C.D.s as additional collateral, the Bank was comfortable with the loan. Management had calculated, if and when the borrower for some reason failed to make payments, the C.D.s would cover five years of the interest cost. In reality, the borrower could not default for five years. Nevertheless, the loan was deemed as substandard by the examiner. The Bank was required to write down the loan by more than $300,000. When the loan was approved in Loan Committee, some members expressed a concern with taking lots as collateral. The committee, however, reasoned that the additional C.D. collateral had adequately mitigated the risk.

Such strict examinations had become commonplace at all of the area banks. The bankers were angered by the severity of the criticisms leveled at their banks by the examiners. Some of the bankers began reaching out to leaders in Washington for assistance.[51]

The moment of truth for Enterprise came at the regular September 2009 Board meeting with the presentation of the recently completed "Safety and Soundness Examination Report". As is customary, the examining regulator, in this case the FDIC, would meet with the full Board to discuss the details of its findings. Management knew from its exit interview with the Examiner in Charge that the final examination report would not be good. Having heard the horror stories from other area bankers, Management was expecting some type of regulatory action. Its fears were confirmed when Management learned of who would be attending the meeting. In addition to the Examiner in Charge, a contingent that included five top brass representatives from the FDIC and Department of Banking would be in attendance.

Generally, these meeting would be of a constructive nature. However, from the onset the direction of this meeting went downhill. The theme turned from one of explanation of the report to a reprimand... like a five-year-old being scolded for wetting his pants. As a group the regulatory representatives were overly critical, and some had addressed the Board in a demeaning manner. The insinuations that the Board had neglected its duties while overseeing the affairs of the bank were not deserved. The blame for the deteriorating condition of Enterprise should not have been attributed solely to the Board's decision making. The regulators never mentioned that Henry County and its banks were impacted by the worst economic recession since the Great Depression. It certainly had to be considered as the major cause for Enterprise's present predicament. The message from the regulators was that the Board had been too lax in granting loans. They made it sound as if the Loan Officers were tossing money into the backseat of every borrower that drove through the drive-in...which was not the case!

The $5,040,000 write down substantially lowered Enterprise's capital.[52] Even with the large reduction in its capital base Enterprise, however, was still considered as an "adequately capitalized" bank. The Bank's Capital Ratio, which was computed by dividing the Bank's core capital by it total assets, still hovered above 6%. With more than $6 million in capital, Enterprise was a long way from being unable to operate. Bank regulators consider banks with a capital of 8% or more to be "well capitalized", 6% to 8% to be "adequately capitalized", and less than 6% to be "under capitalized".

....

Enterprise Financial Statement
2009 - 2010

	2009 ($)	2010 ($)
Total Loans	74,824,185	72,001,332
Loan Loss Reserve	1,942,143	1,471,921
Securities & Fed Funds	17,315,668	5,381,808
Fixed Assets	2,976,948	2,733,325
Total Assets	104,690,359	99,542,745
Total Deposits	95,996,437	94,591,097
Total Capital	5,394,163	1,352,796
Interest Income	4,452,698	3,604,525
Securities Income	170,470	159,521
Loans & Fees Charges	279,758	176,940
Interest Expenses	2,700,686	2,055,984
Personal Expenses	908,610	1,025,247
Administration	1,915,487	1,695,969
Contributions Loan Res		
Net Income (Loss)	(5,661,857)	(4,076,272)

....

As a result of the decline in capital and the number of criticized loans cited in the examination report, Enterprise was issued a Consent Order. The dreaded Consent Order was supposedly a voluntary agreement between the Bank and the FDIC although the Bank had no input as to its contents. It had a friendlier connotation than its predecessor which was called "Cease and Desist". Each had the same enforcement power. There were stiff consequences for the bank and/or those in charge who did not comply with the order.

The members of the Enterprise Board along with its general council reported to the FDIC regional office on Tenth Street in Atlanta on December 23, 2009, to sign the Order. The 19-page document restricted certain future banking activities and required the implementation of specific corrective actions.

The FDIC's Consent Order included most of the same mandates found in the Banking Department's M.O.U. The Board was already addressing those concerns and had begun to make some headway with some of the items mentioned. The Consent Order was now much more severe, as it included specific ultimatums. Failure to comply could lead to punitive action against Management and the members of the Board including removal from service. Consent Orders, when issued, became public information. In order to understand the severity of the measures imposed upon the Bank, a summary of some of FDIC's demands are outlined:

- Within 30 days establish a "Compliance Committee" consisting of Directors to oversee the corrective action activities.
- Within 30 days commission an independent third party to do an evaluation of each member of the Management team and review their past performance.
- Within 60 days add sufficient capital to cause the Bank to be a "well capitalized bank".
- Immediately charge off all loans that the FDIC classified as a loss.

- Make no additional advances to borrowers whose loans were considered to be substandard.
- Within 90 days reduce the concentration of real estate loans.
- Within 90 days prepare a budget to ensure Bank profitability.
- Within 30 days determine the amount needed to cover potential loan losses and add that amount to the Loan Loss Reserve.
- Within 60 days correct all FDIC policy violations specifically the one that required new real estate appraisals.
- Within 180 days reduce the amount of criticized loans by 20% and within 360 days reduce criticized loans by another 45%.
- No longer accept or renew any Brokered Deposits.
- Notify all shareholders of the Consent Order.

There were other non-monetary penalties that accompanied the receiving of the Consent Order. The most damaging to Enterprise was the negative publicity associated with the issuance of the Order. The Order and its contents became a matter of public record. There were also the added costs in the hiring of consultants. With a Consent Order came a number 5 Camels rating and the highest possible FDIC fee assessment. Looking back, it would have been easier to give the FDIC the keys to the Bank rather than endure the grief that would follow. Considering the economic climate at the time, it was extremely difficult to see how the Bank could comply with all the mandates in the Consent Order. Since very few banks had ever overcome a Consent Order, Enterprise was served with a possible death sentence. If there was any consolation, many of the other area banks were in the same predicament.

Finding additional capital and reducing the number of classified loans in the time span required proved to be an unrealistic request. Maintaining adequate loan loss reserves while real estate values were still on the decline was impossible. Further write down of the real estate loans was on going.

As required by the Consent Order, the use of Brokered Deposits was no longer an acceptable means for funding loans. The practice had been previously endorsed by the Banking Department. The Bank had several of these C.D.s maturing in the near term. Without the renewal of the Brokered Deposits, Enterprise was facing liquidity pressures. With the possibility of Enterprise not having enough cash to operate, once the maturing C.D.s left the Bank, the FDIC placed the Bank on an internal watch list. The FDIC began preparations to take control of the Bank, in the event there was any indication of a possible "run on the bank". A run results when a bank does not have enough cash to cover customer withdrawals.

One of the visitors at that Board meeting was a lady named "Pebbles" (Flintstones),...a sweet name for the person that was a member of FDIC's "firing squad". Her responsibility was to prepare Enterprise for a possible takeover if it ran out of cash. The FDIC wanted customers to always have access to their deposits. Her duty was to interface Enterprises' operating system to the FDIC's main computer. From there the FDIC could monitor the daily financial transactions including the cash activities of the Bank. Management was under the microscope. Like in the George Orville novel "1984", the FDIC (Big Brother) was now watching us.

CHAPTER TEN

SAVING THE BANK

Although the regulators had handicapped Enterprise with the mandatory write downs and threatened its liquidity with the disallowance of Brokered Deposits, the Board was determined to comply with the Order. To do so effectively, the Board realized that it needed professional help and engaged a bank consultant named John Kline. John had been the Deputy Director of the Georgia Department of Banking. I was acquainted with him from his many visits to First State as a bank examiner. I had considered him to be a fair examiner and knowledgeable of the inner workings of the regulatory agencies. The Board concluded that the regulators would look upon Enterprise in a more favorable light if a former regulator was assisting the Bank.

As required by the Order, John developed a capital plan, assisted in resolving the liquidity issues, and evaluated the effectiveness of the management team. The Board also engaged other consultants to analyze the loan portfolio, do a risk assessment, and update other policies as required by the Order. With capital deficiency being the top priority, he introduced the Board to Bank Capital Group, a firm that could assist in the private placement of additional Enterprise stock. Representatives from Bank Capital Group and Enterprise met in October 2010. Several Board members expressed a desire to inject additional capital into the Bank through the purchase of more stock. In return they expected some assurance from the regulators that the Consent Order would be lifted. John advised us that such arrangements would not be forthcoming.

By now the demand for stock in community banks was non-existent. Accordingly, the Board surmised that a stock sale would not be well received. The firm's marketing plan was too optimistic and considering its likely outcome, the cost was prohibitive.

John's second task was to find replacement deposits for the pending maturity of the brokered deposits. These deposits comprised of three portfolios of C.D.s totaling approximately $6 million. John was familiar with an investment firm that could handle the direct placement of C.D.s. The regulators opposed the purchase of C.D. pools from brokers where the C.D.s were registered in the name of the brokerage firm. The regulators, however, allowed the acceptance of C.D. deposits registered in the name of the individual depositors, regardless of where they lived. The agent steered his customers to Enterprise, and the Bank handled the transactions directly. These depositors could generally expect to receive a higher interest rate than they could obtain at their own banks. In areas of the U.S. where there was no loan demand, the banks had no appetite for C.D. deposits. Thus, these banks offered only non-competitive rates. All C.D. deposits under $250,000 were insured by the FDIC. Since the stock market was in decline at the time, investors were turning to bank C.D.s as a safer alternative investment. The Bank had no problem replacing the outgoing brokered deposits. From the ease in obtaining new deposits, it was difficult to understand, why the regulators made such a fuss over liquidity.

As of August 17, 2010, Enterprise had rapidly moved up the Texas Ratio list. From 109th the Bank had moved to 18th...not a welcomed distinction.[53] Enterprise was not the only bank to feel the sting.

Saving Enterprise would be an uphill battle. The Board asked Julie Coile to dedicate her time in preparing the various reports required by the regulators. There were numerous meetings with Management and the Board to go over the compliance effort. She prepared lengthy and very detailed minutes of the Compliance meeting and sent them to the various regulators. It was uncertain who was assigned to read them since so many were being submitted by record numbers of troubled banks.

....

THE ATLANTA JOURNAL-CONSTITUTION August 17, 2011

Georgia banks still hurting

Bad real estate loans continue to sting.
State's High Texas Ratios

From FIG Partners

Bank of Ellijay: 1050

First Commerce Community Bank: 864

First State Bank: 634

Montgomery Bank & Trust: 625

Gordon Bank: 615

North Georgia Bank: 565

American Trust Bank: 554

Habersham Bank: 506

Security Exchange Bank: 491

Chestatee bank: 454

Gwinnett Community Bank: 444

Oglethorpe Bank: 426

Peoples Bank, Winder: 400

Douglas County Bank: 395

McIntosh State Bank: 385

Mountain Heritage Bank: 379

Sunrise Bank of Atlanta: 368

Enterprise Banking Co.: 365

Darby Bank and Trust Co.: 346

Park Avenue Bank: 331

Providence Bank: 323

Atlantic Southern Bank: 332

High Trust Bank: 311

First Choice Community Bank: 299

First Cherokee State Bank: 271

Piedmont Community Bank: 268

Citizens Bank of Effingham: 263

Bartow County Bank: 261

First Citizens Bank of Georgia: 250

Farmers & Merchants Bank,

Lakeland: 245

Peoples Bank, Conyers: 223

United Americas Bank, National

Association: 235

Westside Bank: 228

Creekside Bank: 228

Capitol City Bank & Trust Co.: 223

Tifton Banking Co: 218

Decatur First Bank: 213

New Horizons Bank: 211

Hometown Community Bank: 210

Georgia Heritage Bank: 209

Georgia Trust Bank: 205

Northside Bank: 200

....

2010 was a very stressful and frustrating period for Management and staff. The doom and gloom had spread to all the banks. A *Business Week* article such as the one entitled, "50-mile area around Atlanta was the Circle of Death for banks"[54] was not a morale booster. The robust local economy that had been fueled by the growth machine had come to a complete standstill. The banks were now not lending money, either from the fear of regulatory criticism or from the lack of finding qualified borrowers. Many of our borrowing builders were holding unsold houses and/or vacant rental properties and were struggling to meet their payment obligations. Upside down homeowners, who owed more than their homes were worth, began walking away from their obligations. Foreclosures and bankruptcies were very common. Enterprise's number of problem loans was increasing. Companies were cutting back employees to save costs. Unemployment was on the rise. Perhaps, I was in a state of denial, but I was still hoping that the situation would turn around. I told myself that saving the bank was not impossible.

One of Enterprise's largest borrowers was featured in a lengthy news story by the AJC.[55] Excerpts from the article told of then 35-year-old Brandon Robertson's climb from being a high school graduate to becoming one of Georgia's most successful independent builder/developers. Specializing in affordable housing and homes for first time home buyers, his companies enjoyed phenomenal sales. Enterprise had funded lot inventory loans for his company R & B Construction. As a result, Enterprise became one of the many creditors named in its bankruptcy. Brandon had shown no signs of financial stress as his loans were being handled as agreed until the bankruptcy notice arrived. By carrying an enormous debt load, his companies were unable to survive the "mortgage crisis". As a young builder, Brandon had never witnessed a building slump to the degree that occurred in 2008.

THE ATLANTA JOURNAL-CONSTITUTION March 15, 2009

Builder's fall just one link in chain reaction

Boom to bust: Bankers, developers, contractors got rich together, now share the pain.

By: Russell Grantham

Brandon Robertson didn't expect things to turn out this way when he started riding Atlanta's Housing boom 18 years ago. His two Jonesboro companies were building and selling more than 400 homes a year in suburban Atlanta as recently as two years ago.   But real estate collapsed and now the 35-year-old homebuilder finds himself in bankruptcy court.

Like a rock tossed into a pond, the failure of Robertson's companies has rippled far and wide in metro Atlanta:

The developer filed for Chapter 11 protection in February 2008, owing more than $95 million to hundreds of creditors, including local government agencies and contractors. The bulk of the debt – more than $91 million – was owed to 40 financial institutions, including five banks that have since failed.

Robertson had big plans when he graduated from Riverdale High in 1991. He went to work for home builder Rollin Rocket IV and also started his own company. He eventually became Rocket's partner and now runs the firms, according to his lawyers. The Jonesboro companies are not household names, but the combined operations grew larger than most homebuilders in the state, where small family firms predominate. . R & B Construction and Joy Built Homes were building more than a house a day in 35 subdivisions.

....

Meanwhile the regulators were closing banks. Enterprise had ties with the senior management of three of these banks. First Georgia Community Bank in Jackson had opened a branch office in the Ingles Store at Locust Grove. McIntosh Commercial Bank in Carrollton had sold Enterprise its modular bank facility after it had completed its impressive bank office. First National Bank of Barnesville, which traced its history back to 1865, was closed. Enterprise had purchased loan participations and was accommodating its officers with personal loans. Each of these bank closings brought a special empathy for the impacted officers and staff.

I was approached in August 2009 by Kathy Lohr, a reporter from NPR, for a news feature entitled, "When Georgia Banks Fail, Small Businesses Suffer".[56] The story line covered the impact on local businesses by the closing of their local bank. Since our area had become the epicenter of closed and troubled banks, NPR chose a banker from Henry County to interview. The news feature aired nationally on NPR radio and was available to readers on the Internet.

She stated that "More than 30 banks in Georgia have shut down since 2008 — which was higher than in any other state. As a result, many small businesses were struggling because they couldn't get loans."

"In the Atlanta metropolitan area, which is Georgia's economic engine, nearly half of the banks were now under federal or state regulatory orders to raise more capital. As a result of the pressure, most troubled banks were not making new loans but were restructuring their old ones and trying to build reserves. That made it tough on smaller communities."

The story also featured Heather Bledsoe, who owned a store that sold flowers and consignment dresses, that couldn't get a loan to buy her building. She stated "Locust Grove got several hundred thousand dollars of federal stimulus money for streetlights, brick walkways, and building facades." But, Bledsoe said that businesses in Locust Grove were not getting loans. She started her store with her own savings last spring and rented space downtown. When the building came up for sale, Bledsoe wanted to get a loan to buy it, but her bank had failed and others offered no help.

My 45-minute interview with Kathy resulted in 1 minute of air time. I was able to convey the struggles of community banks and their inability in meeting the needs of their customers. I was quoted as saying; "That after so many years of success, we sort of let our guard down when making loans. And there's a price to pay for our actions, and now we're paying it." I was flattered with the opportunity and surprised to have received calls from Texas and Alabama acknowledging that they heard the story on their radios.

Shortly thereafter, a congressional staff member, whose committee was investigating the FDIC, asked if I had interest in providing testimony for an upcoming hearing. I declined…neither the Bank or I needed any more negative publicity.

When a regulatory agency determined that a bank's capital had fallen below the required minimum, it sought a well-capitalized bank to take over the operation of the under-capitalized bank by assuming its loans and deposits. FDIC would enter in a "Purchase and Assumption Agreement" with the assuming bank. In the case of First Bank Financial Services of McDonough, Regions Bank purchased the deposits but not the loans. In the case of FirstCity, no one purchased either the loans or deposits.[57] With the absence of an acquiring bank, the FDIC would bear the burden of settling with the creditors and liquidating the assets.

With the closing of so many banks, the FDIC was forced to hire temporary contract workers. At that time the FDIC had advertised employment opportunities for 9,000 temporary workers. The positions were being filled by former bankers. Some came from troubled banks that had reduced staff as a cost cutting measure. Others came from failed banks. These individuals now found themselves in a reversed roll. Instead of building a banking franchise, they were now dismantling unfortunate banks.

With the closing of FirstCity and First Bank Financial Services, Enterprise had the opportunity to assist some of their disenfranchised borrowers by making them loans to pay off the FDIC, its Receiver. Even as a troubled bank, Enterprise could not ignore the sizable discounts being offered to the failed bank's borrowers. It was difficult to comprehend some of the deals that were being made. Enterprise made a loan to a borrower that owed over $1,000,000 secured by 10 rental houses. The

FDIC accepted a payoff of less than 50% of the loan balance. Enterprise's new loan was secured by the rental houses and a life insurance policy having a sizable surrender value. The collateral appraised for far more than what the borrower owed, and the rental income was more than sufficient to the pay the monthly payments. The FDIC accepted a 45% discount on a $310,000 loan owed by three owners of an auto repair business. Enterprise secured its loan with the real estate, equipment, and a C.D. The FDIC also accepted a 45% discount on a renovated rental building in downtown Hampton for one borrower and a 50% discount on various unsold but newly constructed residential properties for another. All these were performing loans for Enterprise. These were beneficial to and appreciated by the borrowers, but were of great expense to the Depository Insurance Fund.

In addition to enticing banks to refinance borrowers, the FDIC, through its agents, was also selling notes. Enterprise bidded on notes involving local borrowers that were being offered by The Debt Exchange (DebtX). DebtX was engaged by the FDIC to sell notes inherited from the failed banks. Enterprise was the fortunate bidder of a first mortgage on an office building in Eagles Landing at 60% of the loan's first mortgage balance. The note had a solid guarantor and had a South Georgia bank sitting in a sizable second position. The real estate was valued considerably more than the amount due to Enterprise. The transaction should have been a boost to Enterprise's capital. But, unfortunately the Bank was not allowed to book the immediate gain and add it to its declining capital.

When the FDIC inherited foreclosed real estate from a failed bank, it would auction off the property. One such auction impacted Enterprise. With the scarcity of qualified or interested local buyers, the bid offers for foreclosed property were generally well below the value of the property. One such case involved the lots in Crystal Lake Subdivision, an upscale residential-golf course community, which were financed by the failed FirstCity. By way of a FDIC auction, a bundle of these lots was sold to investors for an average of $22,000 per lot. Enterprise had two Crystal Lake lot inventory loans on the books at the time. Some were premium lake and golf course lots. Tom Carson of Peach Appraisal Group had valued the real estate at an average of $65,000 per lot. At the 2009 FDIC examination, Enterprise was required to write down these loans influenced in part by the "low ball sale" of the FirstCity lots by the FDIC.

Regulators continued to press for a Capital Recovery Plan. Realistically, it would have been impossible to approach existing shareholders, friends, family, or others about investing additional funds in Enterprise.[58]

Excerpts from *The Atlanta Journal & Constitution* newspaper article detailed the capital raising difficulties of community banks. My fellow banker, Dennis Burnett, described his bank's difficulties in raising capital. Cherokee Bank was able to raise $4 million. Unlike the circumstances that existed at many troubled banks, Cherokee Bank had a low concentration of construction and development loans. This was considered unusual since Cherokee County was located in the midst of a growth area. The additional capital saved Dennis' bank.

....

THE ATLANTA JOURNAL-CONSTITUTION November 16, 2009

Banks under gun to raise more cash

Stakes are high as smaller institutions scramble for capital.

By: Paul Donsky

Last spring, regulators ordered Cherokee Bank to improve its battered balance sheet.

Dennis Burnette, the bank's president, figured he'd need to raise about $4 million – a tough prospect, he knew, given rough economy.

Regulators have issued similar orders to dozens of banks across the state, sparking a mad scramble for cash. About one – third of Georgia's more than 300 banks are under some type of

Banks under gun to raise more cash (cont.)

regulatory order with most requiring an infusion of capital.

Many potential investors, from private equity firms to wealthy individuals, want no part of a troubled community bank. And some people who want to help out have seen their net worth tumble in the past year and say they can't pony up.

It was a humbling period, as Burnette and his leadership team essentially took off their banking hats and became pitchmen hawking their own company. But the hard work paid off when the bank finally met its fundraising target.

The state's largest bank – Sun Trust, Synovus and United Community – have been able to raise huge sums of money this year to shore up their bottom lines, selling shares mainly to large institutional investors.

In contrast, the state's small, community-based banks are finding it much more difficult to attract new capital. Investors view these institutions as more vulnerable than their giant banking cousins, who received generous cash infusions last year from the federal government.

"It is extremely difficult," said Hans Broder, President and CEO of Enterprise Banking Co. in McDonough, which is trying to raise $4 million "There is just not a lot of confidence in community banking.

The fund-raising stress comfortably in his rear-view mirror, Burnette says his bank is in a position to weather what's left of the economic storm while also going on the offensive to grab market share from its less well-capitalized competitors.

Enterprise was aware of shareholders of two neighboring troubled banks who had temporarily shored up their bank's capital just to see their banks closed at a later date. First Georgia Community Bank in Jackson was created in 1997 and had reached $237 million. According to its former Chairman, the bank had successfully raised $8,000,000 to increase its capital.[59] In December 2008, however, regulators deemed the bank to be severely under-capitalized and subsequently closed the bank. It was the first community bank with a Henry County branch to be closed.

McIntosh State Bank headquartered in Jackson entered into a formal "Cease and Desist" agreement with the regulators in October 2009.[60]

Pete Malone, its CEO, was quoted October 27, 2009, in the *Citybizlist* publication that his bank had plans to raise additional capital to meet the terms of the agreement. This was in addition to the $3 million in capital injected by the bank's directors and officers in December 2008. The employees and management of McIntosh State Bank relinquished over $1 million of their retirement plan funds to shore up the bank's capital. I confronted Pete and asked, "Why he and his staff would risk their retirement?" He replied, "He and his employees would lose a life time of work if their bank should fail." The bank managed to survive for the short-term but was closed in 2011. He lost his investment and blemished his 30-plus-years, of otherwise, stellar career.

The closing of both First Georgia Community Bank and McIntosh State Bank wiped out the only two hometown banks in Jackson.

I always felt the regulators were somewhat unjust in pressuring Boards to raise additional capital knowing that most of these banks would eventually be closed anyway. When board members, officers, and shareholders take the risk to inject additional capital mandated by a federal order, there should be some assurance that the bank would be given a reasonable time to recover. Considering the fate of the other banks, Enterprise would have to survive without additional capital.

In years past, when a bank was deemed to have serious capital issues, the regulators tried to arrange a merger between a healthy bank and the troubled bank. The "shotgun marriage" ensured the continuity of service to customers and the economic stability in the community. In an ailing economy with too many failed banks to manage, the FDIC promoted a "Loss Share Program" ("Loss Share"). As one of the Purchase and Assumption options, "Loss Share" gained popularity during the most recent banking crisis. "Loss Share" enticed interested banks to participate in the takeover program. Under the "Loss Share" agreement, the FDIC absorbed a portion of the loss on a specified pool of assets. "Loss

Share" reduced the FDIC's immediate cash needs and was less of a hardship on the failed bank's customers. In the case of commercial assets, the "Loss Share" covered an eight-year period with the first five years for losses and recoveries and the final three years for recoveries only. The FDIC typically reimbursed 80 percent of losses incurred by the acquirer on covered assets with the assuming bank absorbing 20 percent.[61]

Several banks participated in the program while other banks were being recapitalized for the specific purpose of taking over the failed banks. To a distressed banker, these "Loss Share Banks" went about their business like vultures circling and selecting their next prey. Since many of these bank's ownership and control were vested in the hands of out-of-town investors, there was little interest in maintaining a relationship with the local customers or the community. Their motives were totally profit oriented.

During this period, finding low risk borrowers was difficult. Most of Enterprise's lending effort was restricted to the work-out of existing loans. These included: reducing the installment payment amounts, converting amortizing loans to interest-only payments, or entering into forbearance agreements with the borrowers. In a forbearance arrangement, a bank deferred legal action provided the borrower agreed to continue making a minimal loan payment. The borrower was also expected to pay the property taxes and maintain the property. It made more sense to avoid foreclosure and allow the borrower to care for his property. At a future time, when the economic conditions improved, it was hoped the borrower would resume making his regular payment.

By now, most of the building lot inventory and construction loans were in distress. Aware of the large supply of building lots, Enterprise wisely did not make any residential development loans but did make a small commercial development in Jackson which was never a problem. Through its lines of credit, Enterprise did lend to residential builders.

The difficulties for the builders came from the number of bank distressed properties now on the market. As foreclosures increased, many potential new home buyers were lured to the attractive deals these banks were offering for their foreclosed properties. As a result, the surviving builders were not able to reduce their home prices, sufficiently, to compete. Consequently, the builders were saddled with construction loans with little hope of finding payoffs. Many builders just gave up and defaulted on their loans. Once a bank foreclosed, it added another property to the oversupply of available distressed homes. As the new owner, the bank could expect a loss, if and when, it found a buyer. The market became flooded with foreclosed properties. The properties that could not find immediate buyers were auctioned off by the desperate banks. At an "absolute auction" the winning bidder was rewarded with a terrific bargain.

As required, Enterprise was continually monitoring and evaluating its troubled loans. With each new appraisal, the value of the underlying collateral had declined, requiring an additional write down of the loan. A borrower, who became more than 30 days delinquent with a payment, would most likely see his loan downgraded by the Internal Auditor. As required by the Consent Order, a borrower whose loan was given a "substandard" or worst classification was not eligible for further loan advances. This applied to situations even where the Bank had the opportunity to shore up an existing credit line. As more borrowers began experiencing difficulty, Enterprise's problems mushroomed.

Following the issuance of a Consent Order, the regulators would send an inspection team to the cited bank to review the bank's compliance progress. Management was relieved that at the June 2010 visit no further criticisms were forthcoming, and no additional loans had to be written down.

At that time, the Abbeville office was conducting business as normal and oblivious to the chaos in Henry County. The Georgia farm belt was doing reasonably well. Commodities prices were up, and irrigated land was producing bountiful crops. Peanuts, cotton, and watermelons were the crops of choice in the Wilcox County area. Many also had pasture land for their cattle and produced hay. The more successful farmers, such as our shareholders, the Greens, were large land owners. In addition to farming, they leased their excess land to the smaller farmers. To induce the local banks to make crop loans, these farmers purchased insurance to protect the bank against crop loss. To avoid the burden of owning expensive equipment, these farmers traded a portion of their yield to have the crop harvested. Everyone in the agriculture community prospered as long as the weather and crop prices remained favorable.

My visits to Abbeville were now reduced to once a month. My trips revolved around the board meetings. It was always difficult for local Board members to grasp the magnitude of the real estate loan problems in Henry County. Wilcox County had so few. The Abbeville office now had about $8 million in loans which was nearly double the amount it had when the investors acquired Dorsey State Bank. There were some Abbeville borrowers that had their struggles, but Glenn Dorsey was always able to coax them into paying. I recall the relationship with one of Abbeville's larger borrowers. He was a local farmer who had one of the few pig operations in the area. The loan was well secured by his farm land. He also did some crop farming and raised cattle. He and his wife were very devout Christians and felt that their mission in life was to care for orphaned children. In addition to the three they had naturally, they adopted another 14. Farming and raising such a large family had to be a tremendous challenge for the family. Glenn and I had a great deal of respect for the borrower and were very compassionate in working with his needs. On the other side of the spectrum, a loan to the local public official got so far behind that Enterprise was forced to charge off his loan. Even with Glenn's collection efforts, the Bank was never able to recover the collateral.

The Board received a Letter of Intent from an investor who had expressed interest in purchasing the Bank. The Board met with the investor in September 2010 and agreed to provide his group with financial data. Although his group showed interest, further negotiations never developed.

By now Enterprise was quite ill and suffering from an overdose of non-performing loans. With no immediate miracle drug available, a recovery was a long shot. During my previous banking days, a 4% delinquency rate of loans, as a percent of total outstanding loans over 30 days, was considered high. In fact, First State delinquencies generally ranged between 1% and 3%. The Georgia bank delinquency averages at the time were around 10%. The majority of the Enterprises' loans were not seriously past due, but because of a handful of large delinquent real estate loans, the Bank's percentage had climbed to 30%. Though these numbers were unacceptable, there were signs that the upward trend in delinquencies had reached a peak. The next regulatory examination occurred in late summer. The Board soon learned that its efforts to save the Bank were not successful.

CHAPTER ELEVEN

THE LAST DAYS

The FDIC and Banking Department conducted a joint audit of the Bank in August of 2010. The results of the examination were presented to the Board at its regular meeting on September 15, 2010. Members of the Board, Senior Officers, and John Kline, the Bank's Consultant, met with a delegation from the Banking Department and FDIC. The Preliminary Report of Examination showed that the Bank was under-capitalized. By taking in to account, the additional write downs required by the examiners, Enterprise's capital ratio had fallen below the minimum threshold. If the capital ratio of 1.78% were allowed to stand, the Bank was subject to closure.

By the end of 2010, Enterprise had shrunk to $99.5 million in assets, $72 million in loans, and $94.5 million in deposits. It was a year where Management was continually writing down real estate loans and charging off others. The examination required Enterprise to write down an additional $3 million. The Bank could not withstand the $4.5 million net operating loss that resulted.

In a typical audit of a bank, the examiners would pass loans that management knew had apparent credit weakness, but at the same time would find fault with other loans that management knew posed only a minimal risk. On average most examinations fairly and accurately reflected the overall financial position of a bank. Enterprise's final examination was far from the norm. It was obvious from the onset of the examination that the Banking Department in tandem with the FDIC had intentions of shutting down Enterprise. The decision was probably predetermined prior to their arrival, and the examination was just an academic exercise.

Enterprise certainly had a portfolio full of troubled loans, but the loans that were targeted that pushed the capital level below the mandatory 2%, were a stretch. It may be stepping out of bounds to elaborate on the examiner's treatment of certain loan situations, especially since the contents of a Report of Examination were considered confidential information. My story, however, would not be complete without the reader having some knowledge of the loans cited in Enterprise's last examination report. The abbreviated summary is limited to the circumstances surrounding the loans rather than toward the individuals involved.

The damage for the most part came from four particular loans involving either the disallowance of a loan recovery or the write down of real estate collateral. This is not to say that there may not have been other loans that could have been cited. These particular loans mentioned by the examiners should not have closed Enterprise. Each loan, more than likely, would have been repaid by the borrower in the long-term. During normal times, these loans would have passed with a less severe classification and may not have required a write down. The recoveries mentioned, in most cases, would have been allowed.

The first loan that was criticized was one that involved the recovery of a "short sale" loss of a lake front property on Lake Jackson. The borrower was allowed to purchase the Lake Jackson property prior to selling his existing home. Unable to sell his existing home and experiencing financial difficulties in his business, he could no longer afford the expense of two houses. Enterprise allowed the borrower to "short sale" his lake house and charged off the deficient balance. Later, the borrower returned to the Bank and refinanced his deficiency balance. The new loan was secured by a second mortgage on his original home and a first mortgage on his mother's residence with her guaranty. The equity in the two properties exceeded the new loan amount. In the meantime, the borrower had gained employment and made six prompt payments on his loan prior to the examination.

Since the borrowers had the ability to pay and met the Bank's collateral requirement, Enterprise elected to recover the loss. On its books, the recovery had added approximately $100,000 to Enterprise's declining capital. The examiner did allow Enterprise to recover the six principal payments but forced the charge off of the majority of the recovered loan amount.

The second loan involved a sizable loan obligation secured by several building lots. The struggling borrower had been a customer since the Bank's inception and had made all of his interest payments. At an earlier examination, the examiners had required the Bank to write down a portion of the loan. Since the borrower's other real estate holdings carried a sizable debt, the examiners considered the borrower to be in a weak financial position. Under the new regulations, any criticized loan involving real estate had to be periodically appraised. To comply, Enterprise had obtained a new appraisal from a certified appraiser. The appraiser had determined that the examiner's arbitrary assessment had undervalued the property. Since the borrower was not delinquent, the Bank deemed the recovery of a portion of the charge off as justifiable. The examiners, however, disagreed with the appraiser's revised valuation and required the Bank to reverse the $200,000 recovery.

The third credit involved a loan participation loan purchased from First National Bank of Barnesville. The sizable loan was secured by commercial real estate in Fayette County guaranteed by four individuals. The loan had always been paid as agreed, until two of the investors were no longer able to pay their portion of the interest. A rift ensued among the investment group. The two well-to-do and liquid partners agreed to assume the payment obligation to the Bank, if the two non-paying partners would relinquish their interest in the property. While the negotiations were ongoing, the loan became past due and was delinquent at the time of the examination. The loan was subsequently downgraded by the examiners. Since the value of the real estate collateral had significantly deteriorated to less than the loan amount, Enterprise was required to write down approximately $700 thousand. The fact that the principal guarantor had a sizable net worth and had the means to pay the loan made no difference in the minds of the examiners. Management had not foreseen the large charge to capital.

The fourth loan was a sizable and complicated loan by two borrowers and their company. The borrowers were large real estate investors and developers. They and their companies owned a vast amount of real estate that was carrying a large amount of short-term debt. The loan had not been criticized before and was current at the time of the examination. The original line of credit was secured by various stocks in closely held real estate holding companies. With the decline in the value of real estate and the non-marketability of stock, the borrowers agreed to substitute the stock for collateral that would provide cash flow.

The borrowers had recently sold a large tract of land on Avalon Parkway to the City of McDonough. The City would convert the property to an athletic complex and fire station. As a condition of the sale the sellers accepted from the City $4 million in Impact Fee Credits along with cash. These Credits could be used by our borrowers in their development activities or could be assigned to any builder or developer. Any new construction in the City of McDonough required the payment of an Impact Fee before obtaining a building permit. The amount of the Impact Fees was based on the size of the construction project. As an example, Academy Sports paid approximately $30,000 for its Impact Fee, when it constructed its store on Hwy 20. With the build out of the outdoor mall on Hwy 20 and other anticipated construction in the recent City of McDonough's annexed territory, the need for Impact Fees was apparent. The assignment of the

Credits as collateral would provide Enterprise with a marketable source of repayment.

The value of Impact Fee Credit more than covered the outstanding loan amount, even when discounted. The regulators, however, considered the collateral as inadequate as the cash flow from the sale of Impact Credits was unpredictable and would not pay the loan on a consistent basis. Since the amount of construction activity in McDonough had diminished, so did the need for the Impact Fee Credits. Management argued that the underlying collateral was backed by a tax collecting municipality, who could not default on its commitment. The lack of new construction was a temporary event as several projects were under consideration at the time. To no avail, the examiners required the write down of the entire loan.

Although there were other loans that accounted for some of the write downs, for all intense and purpose these were enough to close the Bank.

The survival of the Bank was now hanging in the balance. At the advice of the consultant, John Kline, Management appealed the aforementioned actions mandated by the Report of Examination. The Banking Department was required to consider the appeal before issuing a final report. The Board had hoped that the Mitigation Letter, as it related to the two large loan write downs, would buy the Bank more time. The letter mentioned the Bank's effort to induce the City of McDonough to repurchase its Impact Fee Credits for the amount owed by the borrowers. The discounted repurchase price could have saved the City of McDonough an enormous amount and would have averted Enterprise's charge off. The City declined; stating that it had its own budget concerns but would reconsider the matter at a later time.

The Board knew that trying to negotiate its cause with the regulators would be difficult. The Banking Department and the FDIC subsequently ignored the appeal. The combination of the four loans contributed to the majority of the $3.4 million charge off.

With no hope of raising additional capital, the closing of the Bank was a certainty. As is customary in these situations, the FDIC sent a full-time representative to "baby sit" the staff. A retired banker from Pennsylvania was assigned to Enterprise to make sure there were no improprieties. She monitored the daily activities and asked to be consulted on any unusual transactions. The second floor of the bank building contained one large conference room. The Bank was able to make her comfortable upstairs as Management had with other examiners. She was out of sight from employees and customers.

At the advice of John McGoldrick, the Bank's legal counsel, the Board met with and later engaged Bryan Cave. This Atlanta law firm specialized in representing bank directors and officers of troubled banks. The law firm charged $30,000 for its services. In the final analysis it was uncertain, what, if anything, the firm could have done to save the sinking ship.

The Banking Department was now showcasing Enterprise to other banks in hopes of finding a purchaser. Several banks had expressed interest. Under a "Loss Share" arrangement with the FDIC, these suitors saw an opportunity to branch into Henry County with minimal risk. In December, representatives from two banks, who had already purchased failed banks in the area, visited Enterprise. They were allowed to review the Bank's financial records, examine the loan files and question Management.

At this point, morale was low as employees feared for their jobs. The Bank had some employees, who had already experienced the ordeal of a bank closing. New Account Personnel were instructed to make sure no depositor had more than the $250,000 in an account. The Bank did not want its depositors suffering losses due to accounts not being fully insured. Enterprise had several large depositors that were bumping the uninsured limit.

The protection of bank accounts was included in the Glass-Steagall Act. Perhaps it was one of the greatest contributions stemming from

Roosevelt's New Deal. By restoring confidence in the banking system, the nation's economy had slowly recovered. The cost of the insurance would be the burden of the banks not the taxpayers. In 1934, the deposit insurance coverage limits were initially set at $2,500 and raised incrementally seven times. In 1980 the limit was raised to $100,000 and later raised to $250,000, which was the coverage available in 2011. Each ownership category of a depositor's money was insured separately up to the insurance limit and separately at each bank. Thus, a depositor with $250,000 in each of three ownership categories at two banks would have six different insurance limits of $250,000.

All funds in a "noninterest-bearing transaction account" were insured in full by the Federal Deposit Insurance Corporation from December 31, 2010, through December 31, 2012. This temporary unlimited coverage was in addition to, and separate from, the coverage of at least $250,000 available to depositors under the FDIC's general deposit insurance rules. The term "noninterest-bearing transaction account" included a traditional checking account or demand deposit account on which the insured depository institution paid no interest.[62]

During Henry County's real estate boom, many property owners took advantage of the high prices being offered for their real estate. Much of this money ended up in the local banks. Enterprise had several large C.D. depositors, who were instrumental in the Bank's deposit growth.

When a bank was closed without a purchaser of the deposits, the insured depositors were entitled to receive their account balances without delay. Depositors would not have to wait until the failed bank's assets were liquidated. The necessary funds would come from the Deposit Insurance Fund. As C.D.s became popular investment choices, depositors began maintaining larger balances in banks. The risk that the depositors' account balances were not totally insured created an uneasiness among deposit customers. At a time, when bank failures were common, it would only take a rumor to start a "run on a bank". There was no reason not to fully protect all bank depositors. It would have eliminated the angst felt by customers doing business with the troubled Henry County banks, including Enterprise. The noninterest-bearing coverage was of little help, as it did not arrive until the end of Enterprise's existence.

November was the final meeting of the Board. As it turned out, it was the last gathering of the group that had shared five and half years overseeing Enterprise during difficult times.

In December, the Bank received a call from the Banking Department that the closing would occur shortly after the first of the year. The advanced notice made for a gloomy Christmas. The official letter followed on December 30th.

It was awkward dealing with customers, because Bank personnel were not allowed to divulge any information about the financial status of the Bank. I particularly remember a nice couple, who attended my church. Because of our friendship, they opened a new checking account on the very last day. The following day, they read in the newspaper that Enterprise had closed. Their first thought was that they had lost their deposit. Needless to say, they were disappointed in me for not advising them of the upcoming event later that day.

It is hard to describe the disappointment knowing that Enterprise would be the next Henry County bank to be shut down. Over the years I had developed a special bond with many of the other bank CEOs. I had been in sympathy with those who had already gone through the ordeal. Others operating under a Consent Order could expect the same. But, for now it would be Enterprise's turn.

In April, Park Avenue Bank, headquartered in Valdosta, that had an office in McDonough was closed. Brad Burnett, the CEO, had served with me on the Bankers Bank Board. He had always wanted to branch in Henry County. Next, came the closing of McIntosh State Bank in June. Pete

Malone, its CEO, and I had banking careers that mirrored one another. He began at McIntosh in Jackson about the time I started at First State. He also served on the Bankers Bank Board. In July, High Trust Bank ceased operation. Burt Blackmon, its CEO, had been a Henry County banker for many years. Burt and his Board had also established a Henry County presence through the purchase of a South Georgia Bank. In October, Community Capital Bank in Morrow was closed leaving Heritage Bank as the only locally owned and managed bank in Clayton County. Kevin Brumbeloe, its CEO, and I had played in several charity golf tournaments. In October, Decatur First was closed. Susan Turner, its CEO, was one of the first female bank organizers and CEOs in the area. All of these bankers and their banks shared common customers and had similar business plans, as territories overlapped. Unfortunately, all of the banks encountered the same fate.

CHAPTER TWELVE

THE CLOSING

Since Enterprise was a state chartered bank, the Banking Department was responsible for the closing of the Bank. The FDIC, the insurer of the bank deposits, became the Receiver.

HENRY DAILY HERALD Tuesday January 25, 2011

FDIC - insured McDonough bank fails

Business Transactions end on Friday, Jan. 28

By: Johnny Jackson

Former customers of the Enterprise Banking Company are looking for other financial institutions with which to bank following the closing of the McDonough-based bank.

The bank was seized on Friday, Jan. 21, by the Georgia Department of Banking and Finance. The bank's main office in McDonough re-opened Monday to provide limited services with limited hours according to Norma Tomlinson, senior ombudsman specialist with the FDIC. The FDIC created the Deposit Insurance National Bank of McDonough (DINB) to protect the depositor of the now dissolved bank.

The FDIC spokesman said the DINB will remain open until Friday 28 to allow depositors access to their insured deposits, and time to open accounts at other insured institutions.

As mentioned in *Henry Daily Herald*'s newspaper article, bank closings generally occurred on Friday evenings, the last business day of the week, after the bank locked its doors.[63] The regulators then had the weekend to prepare for the transition. I received a call from Kevin Hagler of the Banking Department that the closing was scheduled for the upcoming Friday, January 21, 2011. Management learned on the prior Tuesday that the Banking Department had been unable to find a takeover partner for Enterprise. Mr. Hagler gave no official explanation as to why the two banks, which had spent time at Enterprise, had lost interest. But, the Bank's size, the area's distressed economic condition, and the location of a remote branch office were probably the reasons. Without the continuation of business, everyone would soon be unemployed.

The legal process for closing a bank required an official Order from a Henry County Superior Court Judge. As CEO, I was asked by the regulators to sign an affidavit waiving Enterprise's rights to a hearing. Initially, I refused and wanted to go on record in Court to state the reasons, why Enterprise was being unjustly closed. I felt that Management had successfully argued in its appeal letter, why the write downs required at the last examination were unjustified. The attorneys, however, advised against such actions. They stated that it would only be delaying the inevitable.

Once the fate of the Bank became a reality, my tenure as CEO ended. The poor folks in Abbeville lost their Bank through no fault of their own. The thought, that everything everyone had worked so hard to preserve had vanished, was overwhelming. The stockholders, which included members of my family, lost their investment. The employees lost their jobs, and the customers were without their bank. The last day was filled with sadness and despair. The emotions I felt that day compared to those experienced with the death of my mother in 2003.

The "financial undertakers"[64] as identified by the AJC staff writer, included bank regulators, representatives from the FDIC and the Banking Department, lawyers, and police. The entourage assembled in a predetermined area and converged on the bank at 5:01 pm. At the First Financial's closing, that occurred up the street, an entourage arrived in a procession

THE ATLANTA JOURNAL-CONSTITUTION March 15, 2010

Closing failed banks an emotional experience

Efficient and exacting, regulators show heart to shaken employees.

By: J. Scott Trubey

Strangers in dark suits spill out of a convoy of vehicles and walk into a troubled bank branch on a Friday afternoon.

They're not there for some weekend cash. They're financial undertakers there to pull the plug, take custody of the body and then resuscitate the corpse.

But for the people involved, the process of closing a bank is a grim ritual.

....

led by police cars with lights flashing and sirens blasting. FDIC contract workers oversaw the seizure. To the regulators, it was a well-rehearsed orchestrated event...to the bank employees it was a circus.

Shortly after the doors were locked, they arrived...more than 35 credentialed individuals swarmed into the bank. The Staff and Management quickly learned what the word "seized" meant, when armed policemen guarded every exit door and the vault. No one could enter or leave the building without approval from the Official in Charge. He called for an assembly of all the employees; just like one seen in an old black and white movie, when the warden addressed the new inmates. The Bank personnel were given the orders of the evening. For those, who had an appetite, a boxed lunch was provided. The impression was that a trip to the restroom required permission. The employees learned that they would be compensated for their time that evening. Under the circumstances it should have been considered as "combat pay". The Bank personnel were advised to call their families and inform them that they would not be home any time soon.

As in a military surrender, the officers were separated from the rank and file, and interrogated individually. I was the last to be interviewed by the FDIC officials. I remember the lead investigator was extremely polite. However, the entire evening was a blur. I could not recall the specific questions that were thrown at me. I did remember the interview with the FDIC attorney, an arrogant fellow, who had uncovered a title error in the ownership of the Bank's main office property. Upset, he numerated the consequences, if the Board did not immediately agree to correct the problem. In the back of my mind, I knew that the exercise was for the purpose of uncovering information that could be used to incriminate the Officers and Directors.

The Abbeville office, which up until now had been sheltered from all financial turmoil, was overwhelmed in the similar manner. Some 20 South Georgia bank officials and security personnel entered the branch. That count put more regulators and staff in the lobby of the Abbeville office than customers, who would conduct business in any given week. Jim Dorsey later described the ordeal as having a funeral before one's death.

At 10:30 p.m. I told the lead official that it had been a long day and that I had had enough. He graciously allowed me to leave. Other than my brief case and the clothes on my back, everything in my office became the property of the FDIC. Fortunately, I had previously removed my personal items and files. All of the remaining staff were allowed to leave prior to midnight. I returned two days later to sign some documents correcting the title to the Bank's property. I never again set foot in Enterprise. Two days later, I along with all of the depositors, received checks for the balance in each of our bank accounts.

The FDIC retained several members of Enterprise's staff to assist in the operation of the temporary bank. Some served as support staff for another 6 months to assist in the loan collection and liquidation process. The outstanding loans that were not paid off during that period were assigned to contract agents for the FDIC, namely Sabal Financial, KeyBank Real Estate Capital, and others. The FDIC later auctioned off the building and all the furnishings. According to the deed records, a local bidder named Barry Adams purchased the building and the majority of the contents. He paid approximately $459,000 for the building. He later sold the building to Southern Credit Union for $1,607,600.[65] FDIC sold the McDonough bank office for 21% of its cost and 28% of its assessed market value. My friend and former shareholder Ronnie Hammond purchased some of the chairs and the prints from my office. On my visits to Ronnie's office, the prints rekindle my sad memories of the final days at the Enterprise.

In liquidating Enterprise's loans, the FDIC offered payoff discounts to encourage borrowers to seek refinancing. The borrowers, who could not find new homes for their loans, had their loans assigned to a liquidating agent who managed the collection and/or the package of the loans for sale. Qualified investors were allowed to review the loan files and make formal offers. Because of the uncertain credit quality of these loans, many were sold for pennies on the dollar. The purchaser was then entitled to collect the full outstanding balance regardless of what was paid for the note. Most of these purchases eventually resulted in a windfall for the investor but resulted in losses to the Deposit Insurance Fund.

High Trust was the last of the three Henry County banks with South Georgia connections to be closed. FirstCity Bank and Enterprise preceded High Trust. Ameris Bank took over High Trust's Leary operation. However, the towns of Gibson and Abbeville lost their local bank offices.[66]

I wrote a letter of explanation to the Shareholders.[67]

 Enterprise Banking Company

January 22, 2011

Dear Shareholder

It is with deep sense of regret that your Board of Directors informs you that on Friday January 21, 2011, our subsidiary bank, Enterprise Banking Company, was closed by the Georgia Department of Banking and Finance and the FDIC was appointed as receiver.

While we ultimately were unable to save the Bank in the face of unyielding market conditions, we attempted every reasonable solution and appreciate everyone's support and participation in our efforts throughout this endeavor. In particular, our employees should be commended for their efforts in preserving our customer relationships during difficult circumstances. They have earned our gratitude for their dedication and hard work. As a shareholder in Enterprise Banking Company, we want to thank you for your loyalty and support.

As communicated in previous correspondence the banks in our area have been adversely affected by what is generally described as the worst economic downturn in America since the Great Depression. When economic growth on the Southside abruptly stopped, many of our customers found themselves unable to meet their loan obligations. Correspondingly, due to the real estate market conditions, the value of their underlying collateral proved insufficient to make up the shortfall. The losses created by these situations exhausted so much of our capital that we fell below the regulatory capital thresholds and were no longer permitted by regulators to operate independently.

We are currently exploring methods of winding down our holding company

 Enterprise Banking Company

entity. Unfortunately it is anticipated that there will no forthcoming distributions to our shareholders. As this process continues, we will inform you on the progress.

In connection with closure of the Bank, the FDIC issued a press release, dated January 21, 2011, which is enclosed. This release contains important information for shareholders who were also customers of the Bank.

The management team of the Bank has worked closely with the Department of Banking and Finance and the FDIC to make the transition as smooth as possible for the Bank's customers.

Sincerely yours

President

CHAPTER THIRTEEN

A TIME FOR REFLECTION

Once my official retirement began, I had ample time to reflect on past events. Like a coach after a disappointing season, one rethinks the decisions made that influenced the outcome of the games lost. What were the misjudgments and mistakes? Did the quarterback call the right plays? Where did things go wrong? The coaches always do a lot of second guessing, the players do a lot of finger pointing, and everyone has excuses. The fate of Enterprise Banking Company followed a similar pattern. But instead of excuses, I prefer to offer some insights and explanations.

First of all, I was the driver of the bus that steered the Bank down the bumpy road. I was a member of Management and the Board who made the critical decisions. Regardless of the difficult circumstances, I must share in the blame for the plight of the Bank. Although numerous Georgia banks had failed, two-thirds did survive the downturn. Many of those, however, that weathered the storm, were severely scarred. I do not consider bad management or lack of effort as the reason for Enterprise's failure. Rather, Enterprise was a victim of rapidly changing economic conditions.

The investment strategy to purchase Dorsey State Bank was a sound decision. The relocation of another bank to the Henry County market, however, proved to be a mistake. Henry County was already over-banked at the time. There were 20 different banking institutions having 54 offices in Henry County, controlling nearly $2 billion in deposits[68]...not to mention the credit unions. Had Enterprise remained in Abbeville, it would not had been impacted by Henry County's unanticipated real estate problems. In Abbeville, however, Enterprise would have experienced little growth and struggled to be profitable. The shareholders had higher expectations for the Bank.

....

DEPOSIT MARKET SHARE REPORT
JUNE 6, 2006 | Henry County

Institution Name	# of Offices	Deposits	Market Share
FDIC Insured Banks		(000) ($)	%
The First State Bank	6	569,357	26.67
Wachovia Bank	5	229,884	10.77
First Bank of Henry County	2	202,188	9.47
SunTrust Bank	9	178,184	8.35
FirstCity Bank	3	124,498	5.83
Bank of America	3	102,257	4.79
Park Avenue Bank	2	96,794	4.53
United Community Bank	2	77,776	3.64
McIntosh State Bank	2	76,072	3.56
Heritage Bank	3	71,935	3.37
First NB of Griffin	2	71,349	3.34
Branch Banking & Trust Co	2	53,725	2.52
First Nation Bank	2	46,042	2.16
RBC Centura Bank	2	29,797	1.40
Washington Mutual Bank	4	24,385	1.14
Southern Community	1	13,502	0.63
First Georgia Community Bank	1	13,067	0.61
Peachtree National Bank	1	10,047	0.47
Regions Bank	1	4,737	0.22
Guaranty Bank	1	284	0.01
Number of Banks in the Market: 20	54	1,995,880	100.00

Unbeknown to the Board at that time, the hot bed for real estate related opportunities had already peaked, and the local economy had no place to go except downward. Out of town banks had saturated the area with business development personnel scourging for loans. Henry County had become one of the most sought-after banking markets in the state. Enterprise was in a banking environment, where the borrowers were dictating loan terms, rates and conditions...not a favorable situation for an upstart Bank.

Enterprise was a small bank by comparison to the other banks in the surrounding area. In order to succeed, it was forced to compete at a level equal to these community banks, as well as the larger metro banks, that had a local presence. In the process, Enterprise extended several large lines of credit. Although the loan risks for these credits were deemed to be acceptable at the time, some borrowers were not able to overcome the stresses of a weakening economy that followed. In retrospect, spreading more of the lending risks among smaller borrowers, rather than relying on a few large borrowers, would not have made any difference. The survival rates among the commercial real estate borrowers were similar regardless of their size or net worth. Of those who were highly lever-aged, few survived.

One must consider that the price of commercial real estate in Henry County was at an all-time high. As an example, commercial lots on Hwy 20 in the vicinity of the Bank sold for $600,000 per acre. Building lot prices in an average subdivision sold for $50,000 and up. Undeveloped raw land without sewer commanded a $30,000 per acre price. To attract a local builder, Enterprise was faced with having to fund an inventory of at least 5 lots and perhaps two construction loans to be competitive. On the conservative side, the loan commitments were in $750,000 range. Most of the targeted borrowers had existing and well-established bank-ing relationships with other banks. It was a challenge to convince these individuals to move a portion of their business to Enterprise. Chairman Hudgins had success when approaching potential customers by using the 'catch phrase'; "Enterprise had money to lend and needed to make loans." Many accepted his invitation.

Enterprise failed because borrowers did not live up to their commitments and did not repay their loans. In the 35 years as a lender, I had never witnessed the staggering number of borrowers who could not or would not repay their loans. In hindsight, the Loan Officers would have done the borrowers and the Bank a favor by passing on some of the real estate loan requests. But in fairness to most of the borrowers, their inability to pay was not due to a lack of effort, but lack of liquidity. In a rapid growth area such as Henry County, two elements were necessary to support a striving economy. There had to be buyers to purchase goods and lenders to finance these purchases. The same holds true for real estate. When both are curtailed, the economic engine that is dependent on growth stalls. Only those with adequate cash reserves can survive in such an environment. The true character of borrowers was severely tested. Under pressure, some well-to-do borrowers chose to hire lawyers rather than make the personal sacrifices needed to repay their loans.

In analyzing Enterprise's troubled borrower's profile, I determined that many had too much debt. These borrowers were ill equipped to withstand a severe economic slowdown. Even those who had enjoyed several years of increased earnings and had accumulated a cache of assets, began to struggle under the weight of their debt. Most were not very liquid as they had continually reinvested their new-found cash into the next big deal. The Loan Officers, when considering the merits of a loan request, relied too heavily on the borrower's net worth and placed too little emphasis on their global outstanding debt. Many of the borrowers were well known to Enterprise. Loan Officers sometimes let past relationships and reputations outweigh the borrowers' financial capacities.

The evaluation of loan risk was a function of lending and was the responsibility of Loan Officers and Committees. Such risks were measured in part by the historical performances of the borrowers. The mindset of a banker was that if a borrower had paid off his previous loan as agreed, then he was automatically eligible for another. Such logic worked well during normal times but not so in an economic downturn.

Because of the difficult economic times, Enterprise incurred losses as result of some borrower's poor decisions and/or desperate actions. For the most part, the borrowers that followed me to Enterprise became loyal customers. There were exceptions...I was disappointed in those that walked away from their Enterprise obligations without making any meaningful attempt to repay their loans. There was the borrower, who I held in high regard, until he was indicted for sales tax fraud. While in route to begin his prison sentence, his family brought the keys to his farmhouse that the Bank had financed. There was the builder, who was so cash poor, that he failed to renew his builder's risk insurance policy. He had just completed construction of a house, financed by Enterprise. To the disappointment of the awaiting purchaser and the Bank, the house caught fire one night. Enterprise was forced to advance an additional $100,000 to restore the house. Fortunately, the Bank was able to offer the purchaser a short-term mortgage, thus minimizing the Bank's loss.

As part of my final correspondence to the shareholders, I shared my analysis of the borrowers, who accounted for the larger Enterprise loan losses. The loan summary report provided financial details of the unnamed borrowers, whose collective loans led to Enterprise's collapse. These borrowers included individuals, partnerships, and companies. The summary focused on the borrowers' net worth and income at the time the original loan was approved and originated. Based on the financial information submitted and other credit background obtained, all of these borrowers were well qualified. Nevertheless, over the course of a few years, these borrowers saw their businesses fail and their payment abilities deteriorate. As their loans began to get adversely classified, Enterprise was forced to write down the values of the underlying collateral and absorb the losses. There were some foreclosures, but in most cases, the properties were still in the hands of the borrowers at the time the Bank was closed.

Who could have predicted that this group would "break the bank"! These 30 borrowers generated a total loss to Enterprise that exceeded $10 million. Fourteen of the individual borrowers and/or co-makers and guarantors reported a combined net worth of over $10 million. Ten had annual adjusted gross incomes of over $2 million, as shown on their most recent submitted federal income tax returns. Another 6 reported income of over a $1 million on their returns. These were considered to be the elite businessmen and professionals in the area. Initially, Loan Officers and Loan Committee were excited to lend them money and never envisioned the problems, they would create for Enterprise.[69]

Enterprise Major Loan Losses

Date	Purpose	Borrower Net Worth ($)	Borrower Income ($)	Loss to Enterprise ($)
January-06	Land Purchase	5,485,292	1,083,489	412,867
April-06	Builders Line	2,936,276	1,830,519	558,278
June-06	Residential Purchase	5,240,000	230,948	58,600
August-06	Line of Credit	35,908,664	1,985,772	335,025
October-06	Pay Taxes	14,379,216	1,571,969	825,138
October-06	Construction Loans	30,516,166	2,190,498	468,000
October-06	Church Refinance	1,245,000	292,000	48,000
November-06	Lots Purchase	26,826,610*	1,069,412*	466,000
January-07	Construction Line of Credit	2,096,800	142,940	35,329

Enterprise Major Loan Losses (cont.)

Date	Purpose	Borrower Net Worth ($)	Borrower Income ($)	Loss to Enterprise ($)
January-07	Construction Loans	4,685,700	1,274,249	312,000
February-07	Farm Refinance	10,265,500	389,036	146,722
March-07	Lots Purchase	569,000	102,000	63,423
May-07	Builders Line	9,987,500	207,788	580,158
May-07	Builders Line	4,213,885	109,192	260,441
May-07	Builders Line	717,000	(388,433)	117,800
July-07	Debt Refinance	53,726,147	2,495,098	425,235
July-07	Builders Line	44,500,000 *	6,888,000 *	986,889
September-07	Construction Loans	447,000	115,900	170,081
December-07	Construction Loans	951,500	197,544	100,000
December-07	Investment Real Estate	9,379,500	332,177	137,225
January-08	Raw Land Purchase	128,707,961	2,151,956	673,000
January-08	Land Purchase	42,019,000*	4,147,675 *	200,000
January-08	Land Refinance	1,148,948	4,800,000	100,000
February-08	Residential Purchase	43,173,358*	4,462,311 *	200,000
March-08	Residential Purchase	N/A	106,229	74,255
August-08	Business Use	95,439,770	2,916,042	1,016,957
August-08	Business Use	N/A	84,000	34,309
September-08	Line of Credit	119,801,173	15,421,954	1,338,000
January-09	Lots Refinance	4,825,488*	767,838 *	200,000
May-09	Debt Refinance	22,264,988	4,216,217	450,000
*Designates aggregate amount for multiple borrowers				

CHAPTER FOURTEEN

A DIFFERENT OUTCOME

There were several factors that could have altered the fatal outcome for Enterprise and the many other failed Georgia community banks. Prayer did not seem to work this time. In the style of David Letterman, the top 10 causes, not necessarily in the proper order and with explanations, are mentioned as follows:

10. More Latitude in Working with Troubled Borrowers: These were stressful times for borrowers. Most could pay only a minimum amount which came from reserves not from earnings or wages. Banks already had a high number of loan delinquencies and defaults and, consequently, were unable to assist their troubled borrowers. This should have been a time when installment payments were reduced, and principal reductions converted to interest-only payments. In severe cases, interest rates should have been lowered or even deferred. However, any lenience offered a particular borrower was often interpreted by the regulators as a sign of credit weakness. The workout attempt by the Bank would certainly result in a downgrade of the loan at the next examination. Such downgrades would further erode capital. Enterprise was under a deadline to reduce the number of classified loans not prolong or add to the number.

All banks were now reluctant to lend money. Borrowers had very few options to resolve their debt issues. In a hopeless predicament with an uncertain outlook, many borrowers simply gave up. Had the regulators allowed Enterprise to offer cooperative borrowers loan workouts, restructures, or forbearance arrangements without the associated penalties, these borrowers might have made a more concentrated effort to repay their loans. Classified loan totals and loan recoveries would have improved over the long haul.

9. Too Many New Banks: Between 2002 and 2006, too many new banks were being chartered in Georgia. In 2006, Enterprise had moved its headquarters from Abbeville to McDonough. That same year another 19 new banks were chartered in Georgia. Most of these were in the metropolitan areas. The survival of many of the new banks was short-lived as 45 of the upstart banks, that began after 1998 failed. These banks had initial success and were part of a striving Georgia banking industry.[70] Only one bank operating in Georgia was closed between the years of 2000 to 2007. The total number of failures, however, increased to 98 between the years of 2008 and 2016. Each of these financial institutions had its own story to tell. Many of the closed banks including Enterprise were located in the over-banked metropolitan areas. But, others were well established institutions located in rural areas and were the economic pillars in their respective communities.

The end result was that there were too many banks chasing too few good loans. In order to meet profit goals, banks chose to make more risky loans. Had regulators curtailed the number of newly approved bank charters and branch applications, specifically in the South Metro area, the loan quality at Henry County banks would not have declined to the degree, that it did.

8. Rumor Mill: An individual's financial information was protected from public scrutiny by strict privacy laws. But, bank financial information was readily available to anyone with access to a computer. All publicly traded companies including banks were required to disclose to its shareholders financial data as it related to the company's operating statements and balance sheets. The FDIC went a step further by allowing all the various details in the lengthy quarterly Call Reports to be disclosed to the public. The Banking Department, on the other hand, had taken a more discreet position with the information, it received from the banks.

Regulators should have been more protective of the data it obtained from the banks. The banks were at the mercy of the news media as to how their financial status was spun to the public. Allowing this sensitive information to be disseminated in a negative light, proved to be harmful to community banks including Enterprise. Rumors about the soundness of a particular bank created unnecessary angst among the depositors. The publication of "Texas Ratios", which included Enterprise's troubled real estate loan percentage, only added to the hysteria. By 2008, most of the area local community banks were labeled as "troubled banks". Once bank customers became uneasy with a bank, it became more difficult for that bank to retain and attract new customers. Had the FDIC and the news media respected the confidentiality of Enterprise's bank information, the ability to conduct business would not have been such a challenge.

7. Unrealistic Appraisals: Appraisals had become a hot topic with the regulators...in part because of the booming real estate market and the accounting changes. In a "seller's market" that existed in the early 2000s, there were more buyers than available real estate to purchase. Real estate prices were bid up by the demand. Then, as the economic downturn began in 2007, the real estate market reverted to a "buyer's market." Now there were too few buyers in a market having an abundance of real estate for sale. These buyers were bidding down the price of real estate.

Once a sale was finalized, the amount paid for the real estate became an intrinsic part of the appraiser's next appraisal. Known as "comparable sales", the average of these sales established the value of other like property. During periods of "easy money" or "tight credit", sale prices exponentially increased or decreased based on abnormal circumstances. Appraisals, that relied solely on sale information obtained at the peak or at the bottom of the market, were not reflective of the true long-term value of the real estate.

The real estate market in Henry County had become dormant. The primary purchasers of the real estate were those with cash or could obtain private financing. These "bottom fishing" investors were purchasing the properties from desperate sellers, which included the banks. These sales were artificially distorting the appraised values to the downside.

To make matters worse, at the same time there was movement under foot by the regulators to tighten the requirements in the methodology used by appraisers. Their reasoning was that banks were now incurring losses from loans secured by overvalued real estate made during the boom years. Regulators were now insisting that appraisers and banks use more conservative methods in determining the value of real estate. These rigid requirements along with an already devastated real estate market further crammed down appraised values. Property values plummeted to as much 60% in Henry County between 2008 and 2012.

The problem for Enterprise was that each new appraisal became the basis for measuring the potential loss of a troubled loan. Loans classified, as substandard or worse, could expect a write down. Because the Bank was required on a regular basis to update appraisals of its troubled loans, the frequency in the number of write downs increased.

Had the regulators allowed appraisal values to be based on replacement costs and/or average historical values, rather than the most recent "comparable sales", the amount of the write downs would have been less. Appraisals performed at that time were not accurate measures of the value of real estate in Henry County, because the majority were short, distressed, and/or foreclosure sales.

6. Lack of TARP Funds: Enterprise had been in desperate need of financial assistance; however, the Fed and Congress had ignored the pleas from community banks for help. The TARP funds, which could have saved many troubled banks, were not being made available to the Henry County banks. Enterprise had applied for $4 million in TARP funds. The additional capital would have extended the life of the Bank and would have given Management time to work through the Bank's loan problems. It would also have instilled a degree of confidence in investors and shareholders, as they considered investing additional capital into Enterprise.

With political changes in Washington, the focus of the bailout program changed. The funds designed in part to assist community banks was now being used to bailout big business. The Obama Administration chose to use the funds to bailout AIG, Citigroup, Bank of America, General Motors, and others. The small banks were basically forsaken through this diversion. Of $467 billion issued by the relief program at that time, $188 billion was used to bailout only a few companies. The result was the closing of 465 banks nationwide from 2008 to 2012.[71] The shortcoming of this strategy was an enormous cost to the Deposit Insurance Fund. The amount the TARP Program would have paid to bail out the community banks would have been less than the FDIC's cost of closing banks. Many of these troubled banks could have survived.

5. Community Banks Forsaken: Much has been said and written about the National Mortgage Debacle, Real Estate Collapse, and the Bank Failures. Forgotten in the fray was the Georgia's Community Bank Crisis. The shrinking number of the community banks in Georgia received publicity, but little was written about the lack of support offered by Georgia Bankers Association, Community Bankers Association, the State Legislators, and the Banking Department. Too many Georgia banks were closed during this period. By 2016 the number of State Chartered banks had declined to 152.[72] Not that the State Officials had any influence over their Federal counterparts, it was nevertheless disappointing to witness the lack of effort from these agencies in slowing down the number of bank closings.

The Georgia Department of Banking and Finance, who regulated 80% of the Georgia community banks, had the highest number of closing of all State Regulatory agencies. The AJC in its investigation of the Banking Department was critical of the Department's oversight of banks during this period.[73]

....

THE ATLANTA JOURNAL-CONSTITUTION June 19, 2011
Who was watching the banks?

By: Alan Judd

Since 2007, 65 banks have failed, more than in any other state. So far in 2011, Georgia has lost 12 banks, setting a pace that rivals the worst years of the crisis. These failures cost the federal government deposit insurance fund more than $9 billion—losses passed on to consumers through bank fees and other charges. Investors in the defunct banks lost millions of dollars, communities ceded control of local financial institutions to out-of-town bankers, bank employees lost jobs and in many parts of the state, lending all but ceased.

And the Georgia Department of Banking and Finance, the primary regulator of 54 of the failed banks, did little to prevent any of it, the AJC found.

The FDIC's regional director in Atlanta said federal and state examiners rarely disagree. He has few complaints about the state banking agency. "We work very closely with them. We have very good relationships. We find the quality of examinations to be very good."

However, reports by the FDIC's inspector general have repeatedly criticized the Georgia examiners, as well as their federal counterparts, for failing to force banks to correct risky practices or for moving too slowly to tackle problems. Many in Georgia's lending industry, however, still say state regulators deserve no blame for bank failures. Lenders concur in the banking department's fundamental belief in the marketplace and its capacity for self-correction, and in its unshakable faith in bankers as risk-adverse and capable enough to manage their own business with minimal oversight.

The banks' troubles, they say were caused by economic forces beyond anyone's control. I don't think there's anything regulatory that could be done. "We need less regulation, not more."

146

The article further stated that, Georgia by far, was the leader in bank failures accounting for more than 17% of the nation's total. The AJC reporter questioned the Department's speed in reacting to the loan problems that were occurring at the banks. In its defense the Department had been overwhelmed by the number of banks and other financial institutions it was required to oversee. As a result of State budgetary restraints, the Department was understaffed. Some senior leadership had been lured away by better paying jobs in the business sector.

According to the Banking Commissioner, only 10 out of the 291 State banks had a less than satisfactory composite rating in 2006. But, by the end of 2009 just 251 banks remained in business, and many of those were in trouble. The rapid decline in bank equity in such a short period had been unprecedented in Georgia.

The Department should have foreseen the early signs of the asset quality erosion in its banks. It should have been more proactive in warning banks of the impending tidal wave of real estate problems. Enterprise may have reacted earlier and taken a more defensive posture.

4. Arbitrary Capital Ratio: Congress established the mandatory closing of banks whose capital ratio fell below the 2% floor. The threshold was an arbitrary number. In reality a bank had not technically failed until all of the capital had been exhausted. In fact, the limit had not always been at 2% but was raised after the last banking crisis, as a part of the FDIC Improvement Act of 1991.[74] Had the 2% closure rule been in place in the 1970s, many of the well-known banks in Atlanta would have been closed.

Richard R. Cheatham of Kilpatrick Stockton LLP in his Open Letter to Georgia bankers on November 17, 2010, effectively argued that the 2% capital yardstick as the bank closure rule was unreasonable.[75] "Banks do not fail because their tangible capital ratios fall below some bright line. They can continue to operate with no capital as long as they can continue to generate cash. History tells us that in dire economic circumstances given the deposit insurance system's protection against runs, most banks usually can overcome their problems with time and build back any capital deficiencies."

Because of the new accounting rules, many failed banks were holding written down assets, primarily real estate whose values were not being recognized. Enterprise had approximately $2 million more in capital than it was given credit. The 2% floor should have been relaxed during the severe economic recession

3. Dumping of Distressed Real Estate: There was an excessive amount of real estate on the market in Henry County during the downturn. The majority of the community banks were under a regulatory Memorandum of Understanding or Consent Order. Others had their banks downgraded or threatened with some type of regulatory action. Most of the mandates required the banks to reduce their classified loans. To do so, the banks were pressuring their real estate borrowers to pay off their loans. The illiquid borrowers, who were unable to find willing lenders, were encouraged to sell the real estate. As an alternative to foreclosure, banks sometimes allowed owners to "Short sale" their properties. If the reduced price did not attract a buyer, the banks would take the next step, which was foreclosure.

There were thousands of foreclosure sales by the Henry County lenders. These included "absolute auctions" where properties were sold to investors at any price. At the same time, FDIC was liquidating real estate it inherited as receiver of the failed local banks. The sheer volume of real estate for sale and the limited number of buyers further drove down the price of real estate. Enterprise was impacted by the fire sale of the Crystal Lake lots. The after-effect was the appraised value of all properties were driven down.

Had the regulators issued a moratorium on foreclosures and allowed the frenzy of the distressed real estate sales to subside, the real estate market crash would not have been as volatile. Mandating the sale of real estate at the bottom of the market increased the losses sustained by the Bank.

2. Change in Accounting: I recall a comment made by a fellow banker, who had recently had his bank examined. Having had to write down several of his real estate loans, he referred to "Mark to Market" as "Voodoo accounting". There was a big difference between a money center or an investment bank that was holding Mortgage Backed Securities or some derivatives, from a community bank that was carrying real estate notes. These loans were secured by properties in their own backyards and to borrowers who lived, worked, and conducted business in their communities. Fluctuating values of such diverse and different assets should not have received the same accounting treatment.

In previous years suspending "Mark-to-Market" had its share of supporters. Federal Reserve Board Chairman Alan Greenspan urged the SEC in November 1990 not to apply "Mark-to-Market" to commercial banks because their business model was not that of a trader, but involved holding assets on their balance sheet. In 2002 Treasury Secretary Nicolas Brady wrote a letter to the SEC with similar advice.

Mark Sunshine in an article entitled "'Mark-to-Market' Accounting: Kill It Before, It Eats Us Alive" [76] emphatically predicted the dangers of "Mark to Market" accounting. He said, "The change would distort financial results and business decisions under the false cloak of conservatism." According to Milton Friedman, "'Mark-to-Market' accounting was responsible for many banks failing during the Great Depression." In fact, President Roosevelt suspended it in 1938. The practice reappeared in the mid-1970s, was formally reintroduced in the early 1990s, and imposed on banks in 2008. Congress and the SEC should have considered delaying the accounting change until the economy had recovered. The language in the Troubled Assets Relief Program gave the SEC the authority to suspend the rule. It would have been a cheaper way of addressing the financial crisis rather than the proposed $700 billion bailout plan. It would have also saved banks.

Had "Mark to Market" accounting rules not been imposed or at least allowed banks to phase in the write downs over a period of time, the negative impact on Enterprise's capital would have been substantially less. Without the so called "Voodoo accounting", Enterprise could have continued its operation for an extended period.

1. **Subprime Mortgages with Adjustable Rates:** In 1992 President George H.W. Bush signed the Housing and Community Development Act requiring Fannie Mae and Freddie Mac to facilitate the financing of affordable housing for low and moderate-income families. For the first time, these agencies were required to meet housing goals set annually by the Department of Housing and Urban Development (HUD). The government's efforts to make homeownership a reality for every American was a catalyst of Henry County's rapid growth. Henry County was considered a blue-collar county with a population consisting of primarily moderate-income households.

In Henry County many had purchased their new home thanks to the Adjustable Rate Mortgage. Many were former renters or homeowners that chose to upgrade their standard of housing. Real estate agents had little trouble convincing a renter to buy as qualifying for a mortgage was not a hindrance. Thanks to an adjustable rate mortgage, the initial payment would often be less than the rent payment.

In a seller's market, the abundance of buyers added to the number of builders, developers, and banks that were eager to take advantage of these opportunities…Enterprise being one of them. All this demand for housing was sending false signals to Enterprise and its builders. Developers could not complete their new subdivisions fast enough. Builders sold their new houses before they were finished. All of this housing frenzy added fuel to Henry County's already overheated real estate market. Henry County was one of the fastest growing areas in the country. When the "real estate bubble" burst, the euphoric times came to a sudden end. Enterprise became a victim of the real estate crash.

To those who purchased their homes and had adjustable rate mortgages with a low initial interest rates would see their rate reset after the first, second, or third year. The newly-adjusted interest rate, in many cases, resulted in a payment that was more than the homeowners could afford. With no money down and nothing at stake, the new homeowners had little incentive to honor their financial obligations. This was especially true, when their property values began to decline, and the mortgage balances exceeded the value of their homes. Many proved to be poor money managers as they were unable to save money or withstand financial setbacks.

There were also many existing homeowners who were lured to an adjustable rate mortgage and refinanced because of the initial lower payment. These borrowers were unaware of the consequences, when interest rates rose. The initial "teaser payment" in some cases was less than the amount needed to reduce principal and resulted in negative amortization of the mortgage. The mortgage balance increased even when payments were made on time. When these mortgages reset, the monthly payments would escalate to make up for the deficient principal payments. These were responsible borrowers with equity in their homes, who no longer could afford the higher payments.

The massive number of marginal borrowers with unmanageable payments led to mortgage delinquencies, defaults, and foreclosures. Investors were no longer interested in purchasing mortgage pools that contained an unknown number of non-performing loans. Without investors to purchase the mortgages, there was little downstream funding available for the new home buyers. Many willing Henry County home buyers were no longer able to find mortgage financing. As a result, builders, developers, and banks began holding a vast inventory of lots and houses.

Had traditional mortgage products prevailed rather than the adjustable rate mortgage, there would have been far fewer foreclosures and the unlikelihood of a mortgage crisis.

In many ways the regulators made the situation worse. Very few banks could ever overcome a Consent Order. The directives and time lines, that were imposed, were virtually impossible to meet. Enterprise was spending too much time and money on consultants and attorneys. These costs only further eroded the Bank's capital.

The number of closed banks spread throughout Georgia like an epidemic. Very few regions of the State were spared from the carnage. The FDIC's projected total losses from the failed Georgia banks to exceed $9.9 billion. The amount would be absorbed by the Depository Insurance Fund. If the TARP program had been allowed to work, as intended, these losses could have been significantly lower. Had the troubled banks been granted just a portion of the allotted TARP money and given time to work out of their non-performing real estate loans and foreclosures, many of the banks would have survived. It stands to reason that the individual banks with long-standing relationships with their borrowers were in a better position to resolve their loan problems. There would still have been bank failures that would have taxed the Deposit Insurance Fund and would also have created additional losses for the Treasury. However, given the additional capital and a 5-year time horizon to recuperate, many of the banks would have survived.

The list includes the state-chartered banks that were closed between September 2007 and August 19, 2016.[77]

GEORGIA FAILED BANKS | 2009 - 2016

Failed Banks	Location	Date Closed	Cost to DIF ($)
Woodbury Banking Company	Woodbury	8/19/16	5,200,000
The Bank of Georgia	Peachtree City	10/2/15	23,200,000
Capital City Bank & Trust	Atlanta	2/13/15	88,900,000
Eastside Commercial Bank	Conyers	7/18/14	33,900,000
Sunrise Bank	Valdosta	5/10/13	17,300,000
Douglas County Bank	Douglasville	4/26/13	86,400,000
Hometown Community Bank	Braselton	11/16/12	36,700,000
Jasper Banking Company	Jasper	7/27/12	58,100,000
Georgia Trust Bank	Buford	7/20/12	20,900,000
First Cherokee State Bank	Woodstock	7/20/12	36,900,000
Montgomery Bank & Trust	Ailey	7/6/12	75,200,000
Security Exchange Bank	Marietta	6/15/12	34,300,000
Covenant Bank & Trust	Rock Springs	3/23/12	33,500,000
Global Commercial Bank	Doraville	3/2/12	17,900,000
Central Bank of Georgia	Ellaville	2/24/12	67,500,000
The First State Bank	Stockbridge	1/20/12	216,200,000
Community Bank of Rockmart	Rockmart	11/10/11	14,500,000
Decatur First Bank	Decatur	10/21/11	32,600,000
Community Capital Bank	Jonesboro	10/21/11	62,000,000
Piedmont Community Bank	Gray	10/14/11	71,600,000
Patriot Bank of Georgia	Cumming	9/2/11	44,400,000
CreekSide Bank	Woodstock	9/2/11	27,300,000
First Southern National Bank	Statesboro	8/19/11	39,600,000
High Trust Bank	Stockbridge	7/15/11	66,000,000
One Georgia Bank	Atlanta	7/15/11	44,400,000
Mountain Heritage Bank	Clayton	6/24/11	41,100,000
McIntosh State Bank	Jackson	6/17/11	80,000,000
First Georgia Banking Co	Franklin	5/20/11	156,500,000
Atlantic Southern Bank	Macon	5/20/11	273,500,000

Failed Banks	Location	Date Closed	Cost to DIF ($)
Park Avenue Bank	Augusta	4/29/11	306,100,000
First Choice Community	Dallas	4/29/11	92,400,000
New Horizons Bank	East Ellijay	4/15/11	30,900,000
Bartow County Bank	Cartersville	4/15/11	69,500,000
Citizens Bank Effingham	Springfield	2/18/11	59,400,000
Habersham Bank	Clarksville	2/18/11	90,300,000
North Georgia Bank	Watkinsville	2/4/11	35,200,000
American Trust Bank	Roswell	2/4/11	71,500,000
Enterprise Banking Company	McDonough	1/21/11	39,600,000
Oglethorpe Bank	Brunswick	1/14/11	80,400,000
United Americas Bank N.A.	Atlanta	12/17/10	75,800,000
Appalachian Community Bank	McCaysville	12/17/10	26,000,000
Chestatee State Bank	Dawsonville	12/17/10	75,300,000
Darby Bank & Trust Co	Vidalia	11/12/10	136,200,000
Tifton Banking Company	Tifton	11/12/10	24,600,000
The First National Bank of Barnesville	Barnesville	10/22/10	33,900,000
The Gordon Bank	Gordon	10/22/10	9,000,000
The Peoples Bank	Winder	9/17/10	98,900,000
First Commerce Community Bank	Douglasville	9/17/10	71,400,000
Bank of Ellijay	Ellijay	9/17/10	55,200,000
Northwest Bank & Trust	Acworth	7/30/10	39,800,000
Crescent Bank and Trust Co	Jasper	7/23/10	242,400,000
First National Bank	Savannah	6/25/10	68,900,000
Unity National Bank	Cartersville	3/26/10	67,200,000
McIntosh Commercial Bank	Carrollton	3/26/10	123,300,000
Bank of Hiawassee	Hiawassee	3/19/10	137,700,000

GEORGIA FAILED BANKS | 2009 - 2016 (cont.)

Failed Banks	Location	Date Closed	Cost to DIF ($)
Appalachian Community Bank	Ellijay	3/19/10	419,300,000
Community Bank & Trust	Cornelia	1/29/10	354,500,000
First National Bank of Georgia	Carrollton	1/29/10	260,400,000
RockBridge Commercial Bank	Atlanta	12/18/09	124,200,000
The Buckhead Community Bank	Atlanta	12/4/09	241,400,000
First Security National Bank	Norcross	12/4/09	30,100,000
The Tattnall Bank	Reidsville	12/4/09	13,900,000
United Security Bank	Sparta	11/6/09	58,000,000
American United Bank	Lawrenceville	10/23/09	44,000,000
Georgia Bank	Atlanta	9/25/09	892,000,000
First Coweta Bank	Newnan	8/21/09	48,000,000
eBank	Atlanta	8/21/09	63,000,000
Six Subs of Security Bk Corp	Macon	7/24/09	807,000,000
First Piedmont Bank	Winder	7/17/09	29,000,000
Neighborhood Community Bank	Newnan	6/26/09	66,700,000
Community Bk of West Georgia	Villa Rica	6/26/09	85,000,000
Southern Community Bank	Fayetteville	6/19/09	114,000,000
Silverton Bank	Atlanta	5/1/09	1,300,000,000
American Southern Bank	Kennesaw	4/24/09	41,900,000
Omni National Bank	Atlanta	3/27/09	290,000,000
FirstCity Bank	Stockbridge	3/20/09	100,000,000
Freedom Bank of Georgia	Commerce	3/6/09	36,200,000
FirstBank Financial Services	McDonough	2/6/09	111,000,000
Integrity Bank	Alpharetta	8/29/08	300,000,000
First Georgia Community	Jackson	12/5/08	72,000,000
NetBank	Alpharetta	9/28/07	110,000,000

As depressing as the Bank's balance sheet and operating statements appeared in 2010, Enterprise still had the potential of generating cash. At that time Enterprise's short-term borrowing cost was at an interest rate hovering around 1.0%. The average interest rate paid by its borrowers was around 6%. Enterprise's other primary source of funding came from C.D. depositors, who were paid an interest at a rate of approximately 2%. The Bank had a gross interest spread between its cost of deposits and its return from loans in excess of 4%. In such an interest rate environment, Enterprise had a positive operating margin. Even with the inordinate expenses imposed by the Consent Order and other mandates, Enterprise would have been able to withstand the weight of its non-paying loan customers. The risk-based FDIC insurance assessment, extra consultant and attorney fees, cost of excess liquidity and the inability to conduct regular business were expenses that were difficult to overcome. Nevertheless, Enterprise could have remained liquid for an extended time period.

At the time of Enterprise's closing, the bank had $14.5 million in cash, $1.3 million in capital, $1.5 million in the Loan Loss Reserve, and unencumbered real estate valued at $2.9 million. No other business would have been deemed insolvent with similar liquidity and assets. I never considered Enterprise to be a failed bank. It did not fail due to lack of liquidity. As one banker stated "it was appraised to death". It was 2012 before the flood of Georgia bank closings subsided. To have so many banks fail in such a short period, while under the watchful eye of regulators, was an indication of the shortcomings of the regulatory system. Banks were probably the most regulated businesses, so why should so many of them fail?

CHAPTER FIFTEEN

MISERY INDEX

Presidential candidate Ronald Reagan coined the term "Misery Index" in his campaign speeches to describe how the nation's bad economy had impacted the voters. His index measured the decline of American's financial well-being that occurred during his opponent's previous term in office. His use of the index was instrumental in Mr. Reagan's election victory.

On the local level, a degree and type of misery touched every individual in some way or another during the Great Recession. Certain individuals and families had to cope with either unemployment, bankruptcy, crime, foreclosure and/or investment loss. Certainly, the closing of community banks in Henry County including Enterprise only worsened the already difficult times many citizens of Henry County were facing. Without the local bankers, their financial problems were harder to resolve.

The local newspaper, the *Henry Herald*, ran an article the week following Enterprise's closure. An excerpt entitled "Henry Bankruptcies Second-Highest in Nation", quoted the newly elected Henry County Commission Chairwoman, B. J. Mathis. She commented in her State of the County address, "I think our citizens are very responsible, and many of them hung on as long as they could. I think (bankruptcy) was the last thing they wanted to do, but it was the only option left to them."[78]

A side effect of unemployment was crime. Henry County's citizens saw non-violent crimes increase beginning in 2006 and continued its upward rise until 2013. In one of the crime statistics was included the robbery of Enterprise. A lone gunman robbed Enterprise when most of the em-

Henry Daily Herald January 26, 2011

Henry bankruptcies second-highest in nation

200 to 300 monthly, since last July

By: Jason A. Smith

Henry County currently has the second-highest rate of bankruptcy filings in the country, according to a nationwide study conducted at Columbia Law School, in New York City.

Henry has posted high bankruptcy totals for each month since July of 2010, according to Professor Ronald Mann, who is coordinating the project. The study, he said, tracks the number of bankruptcies filed per million homes, in every county across the country.

"Henry County has been in the top 10 every month," Mann said. "No other county has been in the top 10 every month."

There have been between 200 and 300 bankruptcy filings in Henry, each month since the study began, the professor said. He said he is concerned about Henry's relatively small size, compared other counties being monitored.

It's a small county, and that's a lot of bankruptcy filings for a county that size,: Mann said. "It was No 1 in August and October, and No 2 in September and December.

Henry County Commission Chairman B. J. Mathis reported, in her Jan. 19 "State of the County Address,: that Henry County economy has been tied to the housing including businesses for plumbers, electricians, builders, real estate agents and bankers. "That's come to a screeching halt."

"There's absolutely no work."

. . . .

ployees had left for lunch. The robber had approached bank teller, Penny Pollard, and demanded cash. Although he made off with only a small sum in his white pickup truck, he left a lasting impression on the tellers. He was never seen again. It was learned that he had earlier robbed another bank in South Georgia. Most bank robbers are apprehended. They usually cannot resist the temptation of the easy money and will continue to rob until they are eventually caught. Since this robber never robbed again, it can be assumed his actions were motivated by a temporary financial need rather the pursuit of a life of crime.

NON-VIOLENT CRIME STATISTICS

YEAR	ROBBERY	BURGLARY	LARCENY	VEHICLE THEFT	TOTAL
2005	36	365	1,177	204	1,782
2006	144	974	2,251	498	3,867
2007	168	1,090	2,411	444	4,113
2008	167	1,302	3,824	547	5,840
2009	105	1,309	3,464	460	5,338
2010	119	1,539	3,477	471	5,606
2011	126	1,579	3,867	424	5,996
2012	123	1,609	3,943	444	6,119
2013	150	1,362	4,050	426	5,988
2014	144	1,391	4,151	434	6,120
2015	181	1,255	4,161	449	6,046

The robbery of Enterprise paled when compared to the one, that occurred years earlier at the Hudson Bridge branch of The First State Bank. The robbery had special meaning to me since the bank office was located near my home. A gang with guns drawn entered the bank threatening the employees. One robber held a gun to the head of the branch manager, Ronnie Burch, demanding he and his staff's full cooperation. The robbers had hoped to enter a safe where they assumed the bulk of the cash was kept. The safe was always closed during the day and contained a time-delayed combination lock. Since the door could not immediately be opened, the robbers grew impatient and elected to made a hasty departure. For their trouble, they were only able to snatch a small amount of cash from the teller drawers. The gang had parked a second getaway car in a nearby subdivision which was within walking distance from my home. After more robberies the gang was apprehended.

First State's money was never recovered. All banks are required to carry insurance to cover losses from thefts. Since this coverage carries a high deductible, neither Enterprise or First State's losses were large enough to file a claim.

One would assume that once the local economy entered into a recovery period the number of reported incidents would decline or at the least level off. This was not the case in Henry County. The aggregate number of non-violent crimes and thefts continued to rise. The Great Recession had forever changed the social dynamics in Henry County.[79]

The large number of foreclosures had dramatically impacted the value of homes in Henry County. Two AJC articles using data from the Board of Realtors and "Smart Numbers" provided some insight as to the decline in home sale prices in the Atlanta area.[80] Sales of existing homes had increased slightly in 2010; however, 32% of the sales were a short and foreclosure sales. In zip code 30281, which included Stockbridge, the median sales price of a house in 2011 was $71,000. The amount represented a decline of 23.5% from the year before. The median house sales price from 2007 to 2011 decreased by 52.6%. The numbers were somewhat skewed by the number of "short sales" that occurred during this period. Had foreclosure sale numbers been used, the percentage of decline would have been greater. It was possible, under this scenario, that someone who had bought a home in 2007 and paid $150,000 could expect to receive no more than $84,000 for the same house in 2011. In a four-year timespan the homeowner stood to lose $66,000 if he had sold his home. In 2011 home sales had increased in all but one of the Henry County's zip codes from the year before. The reason being, that many of the buyers were speculators who bought the properties below their market values. These investors determined the residential properties to be cheap and could later be "flipped" at a profit.[81]

Sale statistics in adjoining Clayton and DeKalb zip codes were even worse. In August 2008 the Clayton County Public School System had lost its accreditation due to the inability of its elected Board to comply with certain quality standards. Without accreditation, many colleges would not

....

THE ATLANTA JOURNAL-CONSTITUTION January 16, 2012
Sales rise slightly for existing homes

Foreclosure, short – sale purchases noted as 32% of total in December.

By: Misty Williams

Sales of existing homes in metro Atlanta rose slightly in December, reflecting an upward trend nationwide that may be a sign of a market recovery.

Last year saw a big increase in the number of homes sold for below $100,000, many of them foreclosures that were snapped up by investors, said local board president Mitch Kaminer, adding that there may a slight increase in sales in 2012.

....

RESIDENTIAL SALES DATA | 2007 - 2011

AJC June 12, 2012 Data for this report was provided by the Atlanta based real estate service Smart Numbers. The data included transactions for residential properties by county and ZIP code. Foreclosures and repossessions were not included, but lender sales of repossessed properties were. The listing shows only those ZIP codes with a statistically significant volume: generally at least 75 sales in both 2010 and 2011.

ZIP	Median Price in 2011	Change 2010 - 11	Change 2007 - 11	Units Sold 2011	Change 2010 - 11
	$	%	%		%
Henry County					
30228	85,250	-30.7	-56.6	346	18.9
30248	92,000	-11.1	-47.4	331	6.8
30252	127,050	-9.3	-41.7	521	4.2
30253	97,000	-15.7	-43.3	690	1.0
30281	71,000	-23.5	-52.6	726	14.2
30294	56,500	-22.2	-68.9	108	-17.4

RESIDENTIAL SALES DATA | 2007 - 2011 (cont.)

AJC June 12, 2012 Data for this report was provided by the Atlanta based real estate service Smart Numbers. The data included transactions for residential properties by county and ZIP code. Foreclosures and repossessions were not included, but lender sales of repossessed properties were. The listing shows only those ZIP codes with a statistically significant volume: generally at least 75 sales in both 2010 and 2011.

ZIP	Median Price in 2011	Change 2010 - 11	Change 2007 - 11	Units Sold 2011	Change 2010 - 11
	$	%	%		%
Clayton County					
30228	51,100	-34.5	-67.3	283	-17.3
30236	38,225	-15.6	-69.4	522	7.0
30238	36,000	-5.3	-70.3	648	8.4
30260	34,025	-14.9	-72.6	294	0.0
30273	36,640	-3.6	-70.7	312	3.3
30294	54,100	-29.7	-72.4	148	-8.6
DeKalb County					
30294	63,500	-26.5	-63.7	254	-10.6
30038	41,000	-24.1	-68.5	638	2.7
30316	80,000	-8.0	-55.5	382	-3.5

....

admit Clayton County's graduating seniors. The stigma of a bad school system further depressed its housing market, as homeowners chose to relocate. Homeowners and potential buyers no longer considered Clayton County a good place to raise and educate their children. The loss in value soured the old adage, "Home Sweet Home".

The severity of the real estate downturn can be best explained by examining its impact on family property owned by Lyndy and me, three properties, which included our personal residence, a rental house, and a rental duplex. All were fully occupied and in good condition during the period. In 2007 these properties were valued by the Henry County Tax Assessor at $413,800, $109,800, and $137,500, respectively. By 2012 the property values had declined to $298,500, $56,600, and $45,600, representing a drop of 27.9%, 48.4%, and 66.8%. These properties were valued far less than their replacement costs. As property owners we benefited from the reduction in property taxes, but our equity loss was staggering.

For the borrowers that were unable to repay their loans, the misery had just begun. Very few achieved headlines in the local newspapers, but most had their names published in the court's official record. Depending on the legal route, they found themselves in bankruptcy court, civic court, or superior court. All the proceedings became public information. It started with the lender foreclosing on the underlying collateral, selling the property on the courthouse steps, and then suing the borrower for the deficiency balance. The borrower no longer had his property nor the additional money spent in trying to keep it. And, now faced a possible day in court. If his bank had failed, his note was probably sold to an investor for pennies on the dollar. Nevertheless, the borrower could expect a lawsuit for 100% of the loan balance plus interest and legal fees. By now, most of the borrowers had liquidated their remaining assets and/or used their cash to stay alive and/or save their businesses. Many had given up and filed bankruptcy. In many cases the legal proceedings drug on for years. It was an inauspicious outcome for many who were credit-worthy borrowers not so long ago. When it finally came to an end, all that was left was a poor credit score and an emotional scar.

Many local borrowers were forced to negotiate with "Loss Share" lenders when their banks were closed. Noelle Nipour wrote an article in *SunSentinal* about the subsequent treatment of some of the troubled borrowers.[82]

Nipour criticized the FDIC's use of "Loss Share" agreements. With the potential of taking a 20% loss on its newly acquired loans, why would any institution take such a risk? The reason was in the method of calculat-

SunSentinal April 14, 2013

Loss share agreements abuse public

By: Noelle Nipour

In November 2011, I wrote a column about FDIC loss-share agreements and how banks who exploit them were reaping windfalls while prolonging the foreclosure crisis, depressing property values and harming American families.

The FDIC took issue with my column and defended loss-share as an important money-saving tool used to encourage healthy banks to bid on the assets of failing banks. The theory may be fine, but sweetheart deals, subjective guidelines and a lack of oversight has some loss-share lenders engaging in "scorched-earth" collection practices where bankruptcy and foreclosure are aggressively pursued even in cases traditionally and more appropriately suited for short sales or loan modifications. Loss-share lenders have no incentive to negotiate with borrowers and why some lenders may prefer and even pursue default.

....

ing the acquiring bank's losses; generally, the reimbursement resulted in a profit to the bank. Losses were not based on the discounted price paid but on the original value of the loan.

Mr. Nipour illustrated his contention with the following: If the FDIC sold a $300,000 mortgage to a new lender for $200,000 and promised to pay 80 percent of the new lender's "loss", then when the new lender foreclosed and sold the home for $150,000, the new lender was deemed to have incurred "losses" of $150,000. The FDIC would cut a check for 80% of that amount. The $120,000 reimbursement in addition to the $150,000 sale proceeds resulted in a $70,000 profit for the bank.

The absurdity of these numbers illustrated why "Loss Share" lenders had no incentive to negotiate with borrowers, and why some lenders preferred and even pursued defaults. Once the "Loss Share" bank foreclosed on the property, it was not overly concerned about maximizing the sales price.[83] Since the FDIC was covering the loss, many properties were sold at below market

No one felt the misery more than shareholders of the 10 closed financial institutions that had been conducting business in Henry County. They accounted for 23 banking offices throughout the County. Aside from Washington Mutual and Park Avenue Bank, eight were locally based banks. The shareholders consisted of individuals residing in and around Henry County. Many were retirees, who were relying on the stock dividends. The capitalizations of the banks totaled into hundreds of millions of dollars that were lost by the shareholders. The shareholders of the surviving banks saw their stock values plummet. As an example, Heritage Bank, headquartered in Jonesboro, Georgia, saw its shares fall from mid-twenties a share around the peak to a low of 16 cents a share.

The closing of Enterprise had a dramatic impact on the employees and customers of the Abbeville office. The Bank had been a fixture in the community for over 85 years. In a community where everyone knew one another, banking relationships were personal. It was a sad occasion to have it come to an end.[84]

During the Great Recession, everyone's lives was impacted. There

THE ATLANTA JOURNAL-CONSTITUTION March 15, 2009

Move to Henry proves costly

Small-town bank leaves roots, prosperity, then falls flat in metro Atlanta.

By: J. Scott Trubey and Tammy Joyner

As hundreds of customers collected their money from failed Enterprise Banking Co. in Henry County last month, a bit of a different scene played out 110 miles to the south.

People in a small Middle Georgia town of Abbeville rallied around the five employees at Enterprise's original branch, who brought in food for customers as they closed out accounts and bid their goodbyes.

Jim Dorsey and his brother Glenn, now 67, rebuffed several offers early in the decade but felt comfortable with a group of prominent Henry businessmen and their plan to essentially transplant Dorsey State to one of the nation's fastest-growing counties.

Move to Henry proves costly (cont.)

The brothers knew the family' next generation had little desire to run a bank in Abbeville. They needed to sell, and they thought they'd found the best option.

The investors all had strong ties to Henry and deep experience in business, real estate, or banking. Enterprise's chief executive, Hans Broder Jr., was a 35-year banking veteran there.

For a while, Enterprise's plans worked even better than expected. In the first year after the deal assets tripled. Enterprise peaked at about $105 million in assets in 2008. By late that year, however, the global economy tanked and the housing market, which had been slowing since the subprime mortgage meltdown started in 2006 seized up.

Many Enterprises borrowers also had loans with competing banks, and when land and home sales dried up all banks were hit. "The bank did as well as its customers", Broder said.

After last month's shutdown, a GBI officer stood vigil at Enterprise's front door in McDonough as customers signed in like visitors at a wake.

Jim Dorsey said he isn't second-guessing the decision to sell his family's bank, and he doesn't blame the investors who took it over. "These were good people" he said, "and they still are."

....

were those who were victims of crime or became jobless. Some individuals with too much debt were possibly experiencing repossession of their vehicles, foreclosure of their homes, or being sued for failure to make loan payments. Others saw their home values and their retirement accounts decline sharply. The shareholders in the closed community banks including Enterprise lost their entire investment. During the period between 2008 and 2011, Henry County residents experienced a Misery Index unmatched since the Great Depression of the 1930s.

CHAPTER SIXTEEN
DIFFICULT TIMES

During these difficult times, many individuals known to me made the news. Normally, such stories generated little media interest, but individuals and their companies who were connected in some way to a troubled bank found the headlines. One such story had a bizarre ending.

As Enterprise began to receive criticism from the regulatory agencies, the cooperative spirit in jointly working through the problems had deteriorated. Although most examiners performed their duties well and provided encouragement to the beleaguered Enterprise staff, some did not. I had determined that those examiners were better suited for another line of work. However, the Board and I had always had great respect for John Cline, a former bank examiner. By engaging John, Management was confident that he had the knowhow and the proper connections to guide the Bank through the regulatory mess. By now, John had several bank clients with similar problems, as did Enterprise. He was most proud of one of his accomplishments in particular. He was able to find last minute investors to come to the aid of a small troubled bank in Ailey, Georgia, named Montgomery Bank and Trust. Located in South Georgia, the town was best known for its Vidalia onions and being the birth place of the famous boxer, Sugar Ray Robinson. By being saved at the brink of certain closure, the rescue presented a beacon of hope to other bankers facing similar fates.

Enterprise was also searching for such an investor. Director Jim Dorsey called one day after he had learned that John's investor had an office in McDonough. In fact, he was leasing space in an office suite that the Bank had financed for two of its customers, Jerry and David Standard. Aubrey Lee Price, a 47-year old former Pastor, owned what was perceived to be a successful investment company. He had assembled a group who injected capital into the South Georgia bank. I immediately made several calls to Mr. Price, none of which were ever returned.

To everyone's surprise, the Board learned later that Mr. Price was the operator of a Madoff-type Ponzi scheme. He had used his clients' money to capitalize the Montgomery Bank and Trust. Once in control he turned his efforts into soliciting others in the community to rally behind the bank and purchase stock. The bank made national news as one of the best "turn around stories" for a troubled bank. Since having obtained the confidence of the Board, Mr. Price with knowledge of securities, was assigned the management of the bank's investment portfolio. It was not long before he converted the bank's securities into cash for his personal use.[85]

....

THE ATLANTA JOURNAL-CONSTITUTION April 24, 2014
Charges added against ex-banker

Fraud counts rise to 17 against man accused of embezzling $21 million.

By: J. Scott Trubey

Aubrey Lee Price, an investment advisor and preacher, is accused of embezzling more than $21 million from Montgomery Bank & Trust, a small bank in the town of Ailey. Price and a group of investors from his advisory business had pumped $10 million into the bank to save in late 2010.

Prosecutors said Price took control of the bank's securities portfolio and diverted money from bank reserves, then lost it in speculative trading and other investments.

Price separately is accused in a civil case of misappropriating funds from clients in his investment business.

In June 2012, Price disappeared and the bank failed the following month. In suicide notes sent to his family and associates, Price admitted to misappropriating money and producing false financial statements in frenzied attempts to make back heavy losses.

He was seen boarding a ferry in Key West, Fla, and later declared dead by Florida court. Price was arrested on Dec. 31 near Brunswick, Ga., following a traffic stop.

In June 2012 Mr. Price went missing after sending suicide notes to his friends and family. He boarded a ferry from Key West en route to Fort Meyers, Florida. Though his body was never found, the married, father-of-four was officially pronounced dead six months later, believed to have jumped off the ferry and drowned in the ocean. Mr. Price faked his own death only to resurface two years later. He is now serving a 30-year prison sentence. Montgomery Bank & Trust was closed in 2012, and many trusting individuals lost their life savings. Enterprise and its Board could have easily become victims had it been able to reach the nefarious Mr. Price. The AJC published several articles of Mr. Price's escapades.

Then, there was my banking colleague, Mark A. Conner. He was the former president of FirstCity Bank, which was closed by the regulators in 2009. He was sentenced for his role in a multi-million-dollar conspiracy to defraud his bank in Stockbridge. Conner was initially indicted March 16, 2011, on 12 counts of bank fraud. He later concealed in his personal bankruptcy petition the fact, that he had hidden cash in the Cayman Islands. Mark was 46 at that time and was sentenced to a 12-year prison term and ordered to pay a hefty restitution to the FDIC and victim banks.

Mark and his senior loan officer recommended certain loan requests to FirstCity's Loan Committee and Board of Directors on behalf of "straw borrowers." According to J. P. Evans, one of the Directors, "The Board had no knowledge that the loan proceeds had actually gone to Mark or that he profited in the deals." When the straw borrower failed to make payments and could not be located, the loans went into default. FirstCity later foreclosed and incurred substantial losses. To compound the deceit, Mark also sold participations in these bad loans to other community banks, that also suffered losses.

After Mark was charged with bank fraud, he fled to the Turks and Caicos Islands in the West Indies. The FBI coaxed Mark to return to the U.S. on the pretense that some money was waiting for him. As a condition, he would have to appear in person and sign for the funds. Federal agents were waiting for him at the Miami International Airport.[86]

As a lending officer, one is sometimes tempted by the easy access to money. Whether it is a personal need, the desire to keep up with the Joneses, or the envy from watching others profit from their ventures, the temptation can be hard to ignore. The intention was always to undo the act or replace the funds before someone discovered the wrongdoing. Mark allowed his temptations to get the better of him. Mark and his cohort were the only area bankers who personally condemned their bank to failure through their deceitful activities.

When investment ventures went bad, it became commonplace for the unhappy investors to look for someone to blame. Many times, they sued the organizer of the deal. This happened to a successful businessman and bank customer named Shailendra, Shi, as his friends called him. As Enterprise needed to find different and more diverse borrowers, other than those in building and development, it reached out to Shi for help. He had been able to assemble several groups of doctors and professionals, who would pool their funds and purchase real estate. Many of his ventures required bank financing. These deep-pocketed individuals would add diversity to the Bank's loan portfolio.

The AJC published several articles about Shi's disputes with some of his investors.[87] Shi had an interesting past as he came to Atlanta from India to study engineering and graduated from Georgia Tech in 1971. He later found employment as an engineer for the Clayton County Transportation Department. He bought real estate and build office buildings for some of his immigrant friends and was able to build a network of investors. During the booming real estate days in Clayton and Henry Counties, his investment groups made lots of money. Over the years, Shi accumulated an impressive resume, gained many political connections, and had bank participations. Shi organized the Peach State Bank in Riverdale, Georgia, and served on the Board of Directors. He also served on the Advisory Board for First Bank of Georgia. In 1998 Shi was appointed to the Georgia Regional Transportation Authority (GRTA) by Governor Barnes. Shi was appointed to the Board of Georgia Tech's College of Engineering. With Shi's credentials and connections, he was an obvious source to help upgrade Enterprise's commercial loan portfolio.[88]

....

THE ATLANTA JOURNAL-CONSTITUTION January 28, 2011
Land deals crumble into cries of fraud

Developer says crash to blame for investors' tens of millions in losses.

By: J. Scott Trubey and Bill Torpy

In August 2004, a small group of investors met in the conference room of a doctor's office to chart a bold course in the wide-open Atlanta commercial real estate game.

Heading the meeting was Shi Shailendra, an India-born man with an infectious confidence and long track record of forging relationships.

Along the way, they were going to make a lot of money.

Those dreams of riches are now the boilerplate for a series of lawsuits filed by Sabadia and others alleging Shailendra sold them a false bill of goods, defrauding them and others of millions of dollars. The suits, filed over the past few weeks, claim Shailendra frequently switched around assets and corporations to confuse his partners while using their investments as his own "personal piggy bank."

Shailendra, in turn, last week countersued, saying his former partners are disgruntled investors, who have embarked on a year long mission to smear him and his decades of service to the community.

"When things go bad, people start pointing fingers at each other," he said. "But this has more vitriol and bile to it."

An Indian immigrant and a cardiologist who has known Shailendra for three decades, said his friend is the embodiment of the American dream.

He came from a humble family. You have to prove yourself and work hard and pull yourself up the rungs of the ladder, said Dr. Mohan. "He built a large network over time. That's how he became successful.

....

171

THE ATLANTA JOURNAL-CONSTITUTION January 28, 2011
Feud heats up in land dealings

Legal filings are furious as developer is accused of defrauding investors.

By: J. Scott Trubey and Bill Torpy

Atlanta developer Shi Shailendra, a longtime player in civic and political circles, is embroiled in a legal war with investors who claim he defrauded them of millions they poured into real estate deals he ran.

Among the plaintiffs: Atlanta physician Dr. Ishtiaq Khan and his brother-in-law, Rahim Sabadia. According to a 2004 business plan included in lawsuits against Shailendra, the investing partners sought to build a $1 billion empire, with each partner increasing his net worth by $100 million over a decade.

The partners bought a major tract in Henry County off Jodeco Road in anticipation of development of a major shopping center, property for development in Florida and in Midtown Atlanta.

The lawsuit includes an affidavit filed by Khan's ex-wife. In it she said the investors set up the partnership giving Shailendra oral power of attorney to act on their behalf, and vouched for Shailendra's claims in his lawsuit about other aspects of the partnership.

....

In 2010 Management got wind that several investors were unhappy with Shi. He was in all of the ventures as partner or as the real estate broker and was responsible for managing the properties and controlling the funds. As the opportunities to resale these investment properties became more difficult, Shi used what monies that were at his disposal to make the bank payments and pay related expenses. Sometimes it involved monies that belonged to a different partnership other than the one, that owned the money. Needless to say, this infuriated some investors, as they used the commingling of funds as reason to sue him. Not all of the investors joined in the litigation. Many were in support of Shi because they trusted him and had benefited from past deals.

Since Enterprise had made loans that included some of the plaintiffs in the lawsuit, Management was worried that Enterprise would be named in the lawsuit. Its greater concern was that the borrowers would retaliate against Shi and not repay their loans…at the time the bank did not need more criticized loans. Fortunately, Enterprise never became a party in the suit, and no one was asked to testify. Instead, the privilege of being a defendant in a lawsuit went to another local bank. Needless to say, the various lawsuits had created quite a mess for Shi that took a while to unravel.

Attorney's law practices generally benefited from hard economic times because of the increased number of litigations. Smith Welch & Brittain was Henry County's oldest and largest law firm. Enterprise had relied on the firm for real estate closings, and the firm had many of the Bank's customers as clients. Buddy Welch, the senior partner, was admired for his courtroom skills. He and his firm represented a number of public sector clients, including the Henry County Board of Education, Henry County Water Authority, several city governments, and a host of influential businesses and individuals.

Excerpts from an AJC article dated February 2011 reported on a FDIC lawsuit against Smith Welch & Brittain LLP and one of its partners, Mark Brittain.[89] The suit alleged that the law firm was negligent in its closings of large real estate loans for Neighborhood Community Bank (NCB) in Newnan which contributed to its collapse in 2009. The FDIC accused in particular, partner Mark Brittain, of legal malpractice by closing loans for NCB while also representing Jeff Grant, a developer client. Jeff had apparently inflated and overstated to the bank the value of the properties that he

....

THE ATLANTA JOURNAL-CONSTITUTION February 9, 2011
Feds sue law firm in bank collapse.

FDIC files civil lawsuit alleging malpractice.

Experts predict more cases as insurance fund seeks to recover losses.

By: J. Scott Trubey

Federal regulators are suing a prominent Henry County law firm in connection with a bank failure, reflecting the government's widening legal efforts to recoup losses from Georgia's banking meltdown.

Feds sue law firm in bank collapse. (cont.)

The civil lawsuit against Smith Welch & Brittain and one of its partners, J. Mark Brittain, alleges malpractice in Brittain's handling of certain loans that Neighborhood Community Bank made to a Henry developer from 2005 to 2007.

Christine Mast, an Atlanta attorney representing Brittain and his firm, said in an e-mail that Neighborhood Community was to blame for its failure and that the loans in question "were at risk for default from the beginning. "The FDIC, she added, was seeking out "deep pockets" from which to recover some of its losses.

The FDIC lawsuit claims the bank hired Brittain to process loan documents for land purchases by Henry developer Jeff Grant. Brittain had previously, and also during the time of loans, served as a lawyer for Grant and companies he owned.

The lawsuit says Grant misrepresented the price of property he wanted to buy.

In three instances, Grant obtained loans using an inflated property price and used the amount over the actual purchase price as collateral to the bank and put some of the funds into various companies he controlled.

....

was acquiring. The excess cash obtained at the loan closing was diverted to his companies or himself. In one particular loan, Jeff was required to pledge a C.D. as additional collateral. The inflated purchase allowed the funds to come from the loan proceeds and not from Jeff.

The FDIC's lawyers contended that had the Neighborhood Community Bank known of the scheme, it would have ceased doing further business with Jeff before it incurred the eventual losses. Down payment or not… NCB had obtained an appraisal that justified its loan decision. Furthermore, had the Henry County real estate market remained strong, the proceeds from the lot sales would have repaid to the bank. Even, the most conservatively financed real estate developments were under water at that time. Nevertheless, ProAssurance, the insurer, and FDIC settled the suit.

Enterprise and some of its Board members were not spared from negative publicity. On August 28, 2011, Russell Grantham wrote a scathing article in the AJC entitled "Silverton Rapid Rise and Fall". [90]

....

THE ATLANTA JOURNAL-CONSTITUTION August 28, 2011
Silverton's rapid rise and fall

Money no object when it came to its growth

The effects of its failure on partner lenders is detailed in lawsuits.

By: Russell Grantham

The bank grew from $1.7 billion in assets in 2005 to $4.2 billion by early 2009.

Much of this growth came from Silverton's "participation" business. Acting like an investment banker, Silverton took on loans that were too large for community bank members to handle alone, the divided them into smaller pieces that it sold to other members, usually keeping part for itself.

Often when it came to verifying the loan properties' values and the borrowers' finances, Silverton dropped the ball, the FDIC said.

In 2006, for instance, Silverton put together a $9.3 million loan to three directors of Enterprise Banking Co. in McDonough, including a former Silverton director, for 643 acre development in Henry County.

Such conflicts of interest should have stopped the loan from being made, the FDIC said.

Enterprise Banking Co. the lead bank for that participation, failed in January.

....

Mr. Grantham cited a loan made to some of the Directors of Enterprise as a reason for Silverton's (formerly The Bankers Bank) collapse. The article provided a detailed account of Silverton's failure. One particular loan transaction that resulted in a loss to Silverton was mentioned. Because the writer did not investigate or verify the information his sources provided him, many of his details and assumptions were incorrect. A loan was made to three Directors of Enterprise Banking Company, one of the borrowers was also a former Director of The Bankers Bank. The reference to a former Director was me, now 10 years removed from the bank. The partners did obtain a loan to develop an industrial 204-acre tract. The loan was subsequently paid as agreed. As a minority stakeholder in the project, I was not a guarantor of the loan in question.

At the time the loan was granted, the property appraised for significantly more than the loan amount. There had been several sales that justified the evaluation. This section of the Westridge Development was the home of Enterprise Bank and the distribution centers for Crown Distribution, Home Depot, and John Deere. The Westridge mixed-use development was then and is still one of the elite commercial projects in Henry County.

The press enjoyed embellishing the travails of banks and those individuals, who had a connection to a failed bank. There were those who were guilty of fraud and had illegally enriched themselves as in case of Aubrey Price and Mark Conner. And, there were those who had the misfortune of handling real estate deals for associates and/or clients that resulted in financial losses. In the case of Shailendra and Mark Brittain, the lawsuits would never have occurred in normal times, but this was the Great Recession. The legal battles blemished their professional careers. As for me, I was portrayed as an unethical banker because of my prior association with The Bankers Bank now Silverton.

Since inflammatory news accounts such as these were written to gain readership, many times they distorted or exaggerated the facts. Whether true or not, the damage done to the individual's reputation was irreversible. Bankers were already ranked fairly low on the "trustworthy scale". The negative newspaper articles probably pushed them further down the scale.

The greatest misfortune during this period was not from a financial circumstance but the tragic loss of life. Doug Coker was a long-time Bank customer and friend. Doug had been a sales rep for a company that sold bank supplies and equipment. He routinely called on financial institutions...which brought him to my office, while I was at First State. It was at one of those visits that he became acquainted with Judy Phillips, who was my secretary. Judy had been my high school classmate and was a long-time employee at First State. A relationship developed, whereby Judy and Doug later married in 1984.

Doug had a keen interest in banking and had served as a director of a newly chartered community bank located on North Henry Blvd near the Hwy 138 intersection. The bank was subsequently purchased by Wachovia. Once Enterprise opened, it continued to assist Doug with the financing of his real estate investments. During his visits there were many discussions about the plights of the Henry County banks, Washington politics, and the numerous bank regulations. Doug recognized the importance of the community banks and had a negative opinion toward those, who had contrary views.

On one particular visit, Doug mentioned his desire to package his residential properties into a government-backed program, that would make his rentals available to low-income individuals. He had learned that such programs were available and was searching for a contact person. He needed a consultant that could help him navigate through the complicated paperwork process.

Although I saw less of Doug and Judy after Enterprise closed, I nevertheless missed the personal relationship we had shared. Doug was a caring, generous, and loving person especially to Judy. And, I always valued his advice and friendship. It was hard to grasp what happened to Doug a short time later.

Tuesday of March 13, 2012, was a typical morning for the Cokers. Both left that morning for work. Doug had a meeting that day with a person, who was assisting him in the creation of a charitable foundation, that allowed the transfer of some of his houses to low-income families. Since Doug had always stayed in touch with Judy as to his whereabouts, she became concerned when she was unable to reach him later that day. When he did not return that evening, she filed a missing person report which led to a BOLO (Be On the LookOut) alert.

Other than a supposed meeting, the detective had little to go on in determining what happened to Doug. Knowing that Doug had a cell phone, the detective "pinged" the surrounding cell towers to determine if, where, and when his cell phone might have been used. To his surprise and with further investigation, he determined that a call was made from his cell phone in Macon, Georgia. The detective discovered that the call was made from a McDonald's restaurant on Bass Road, and the number belonged to Pamela Moss.

The detective, knowing that Mrs. Moss had talked to Doug the day of his disappearance, decided to question her. Mrs. Moss stated that she had been late in arriving for the scheduled meeting, but had met with Doug later that day. She stated that she had no knowledge as to where he was headed after the meeting. During the interview Mrs. Moss admitted that Doug had paid her $85,000 to establish the non-profit organization. She had assured him she was moving forward with her efforts and that Doug seemed satisfied with her progress. Doug's e-mail records, however, told a different story as he had made numerous requests for the refund of his money. It appeared that Doug was probably meeting Mrs. Moss to demand the return of his money.

Doug now had been missing for four days. The detective decided it was time to talk with Mrs. Moss again. He had hoped to find her at home in Jones County, but she was not there. While inspecting the grounds, he noticed a Kroger receipt lying on the ground that had apparently fallen out of the garbage container. The receipt was dated the same day as Doug's disappearance and led to the viewing of videos from the store's surveillance cameras. She was observed buying two bottles of bleach and yellow gloves…a suspicious purchase considering the circumstances.

The detective made a second trip to Mrs. Moss's residence. She again was not at home, but this time he detected a foul odor at the rear of the house. Underneath a plastic tarp covered with roofing shingles and lime was a body. The search was over...it was Doug. The medical examiner later testified that Doug was struck several times with a hammer. Even though, the killer tried to cover up the crime, detectives found sufficient evidence to identify the house as the crime scene. They later arrested and charged Mrs. Moss with the murder of Doug Coker.

As the trial unfolded, it was obvious that Mrs. Moss had no intentions of creating a foundation for Doug as she had promised. As Doug was beginning to suspect...Mrs. Moss was a con artist. Once he began demanding the return of his money, she decided to silence him. The call to Doug at McDonald's was intended to lure him to her house.

The jurors found Mrs. Moss guilty. The Judge sentenced her to life in prison without parole. Her sentence was deservingly harsh. The Judge had taken into consideration the fact that Mrs. Moss had previously pleaded guilty and served time for the fatal poisoning of her mother.[91]

As a tribute to Doug, a Resolution was passed in the Georgia Senate honoring his memory and contributions to his family and community. The financial miseries encountered by Henry Countians paled as compared to the grief and sorrow experienced by Judy and the Coker family.

CHAPTER SEVENTEEN

THE AFTERMATH

My introduction to banking began in January 1971. Paul Christenberry, CEO of First State, hired me to replace Loan Officer, Mack Hill, who had left the bank to purchase the old McDonough Credit Bureau. The bureau tracked the payment records of consumers in and around Henry County and was a source for the local banks and businesses to verify a customer's credit history. Stockbridge was growing and transitioning into a suburban community. First State was desperately in need of a Loan Officer.

I received a crash course in how to make loans and witnessed first-hand how a small bank operated. Credit decisions were based for the most part on the customer's background and reputation. Most customers were local and well known in the community. Most loans were of the consumer variety and were generally collateralized. The bank made short-term real estate, equipment, and small business loans. Credit Life and Disability Insurance was required on all consumer loans. A one-page application was all that was required, while financial statements were seldom requested and not considered necessary. These loans were calculated using the "rules of 78's method" rather than the "simple interest method" as used today. The old method gave the bank a higher return.

Before the introduction of computers and copy machines, documents were simple and many times hand written. Carbon paper was used to produce duplicate copies. Loan payments were posted manually on ledger cards. Bookkeeping relied on a 24-pocket Burroughs proof machine that operated like a sorter. Once the information was inputted onto the keyboard, the transaction ticket found its way to a pocket. The proof machine read the routing codes on the tickets, sent the tickets to individual pockets and tabulated pocket totals. The tickets in the loan transaction pocket were sent to me for balancing. Savings/checking transactions and general ledger tickets were sent to other appropriate departments. Tellers were required to reconcile their cash balances before they could leave for the day. There were only a dozen full and part-time employees at First State's only office, which was located on Highway 42, now North Henry Boulevard, in Stockbridge. The employees were a close-knit group. Everyone arrived at 8:00 a.m. and seldom left before 6:00 p.m. On regular days, the bank was open to the public from 9:00 a.m. to 4:00 p.m., closed all day on Wednesdays, and opened a half day on Saturdays.

Check clearing required the bank to courier foreign check items (those from out of town banks) to the Atlanta Federal Reserve. The Atlanta Fed in turn sent the check items to the appropriate regional Fed offices. The check items were then sent to the issuing banks for credit. A check written on a California bank and deposited at First State had taken up to 10 days to clear. Banking was simpler and more hands-on. It seemed that the work environment was more relaxed and less stressful.

In the years that followed, bank operations became more complex. It was an exciting time to be a part of the evolution of the computer, introduction of the credit and debit cards, and the Internet. The information age radically changed how banks delivered service. With a cell phone, one could bank with a financial institution a thousand miles away. Loans could be obtained electronically, and funds transferred within seconds. I witnessed more modernization of the banking process during the timespan of my banking career than had been achieved in all the years prior.

I can take pride in my life's work as a banker. Enterprise was to be the culmination of my past experiences and knowledge in the management of a bank. The legacy that I had envisioned was not meant to be. I had played a major part in the organization and management of Enterprise. As I reflect back…I consider my involvement in the creation of the bank as an enlightening experience. One from which I learned many lessons and have no regrets.

The AJC and the *Henry Herald* each published stories about Enterprise's closing. In addition to the stigma of having managed a bank that failed, I would have to cope with the loss of my investment dollars in Enterprise. Although Management and the Board did not do anything wrong, the threat of criminal or civil action against the Directors and Officers was a realistic concern. The Board had decided not to purchase Directors & Officers Liability Insurance coverage, which would have insulated participants from the expense stemming from a lawsuit. The premium was simply outrageous. Therefore, the cost of a legal defense would have to come from Board members and Officer's personal funds.

Excerpts from the AJC article in 2012 entitled "Failed banks pay $27.3 million in settlements" heightened the Board's concerns as the FDIC was determined to seek repatriation from the Bank Directors. According to the article, Georgia had the highest number of failed bank lawsuits (25).[92]

....

THE ATLANTA JOURNAL-CONSTITUTION September 4, 2010
Failed banks pay $27.3M in settlements

Agreements maximize amounts of money returned to FDIC

By: Arielle Kass

Bank directors and officers, lawyers and insurers involved in the demise of 11 failed Georgia banks have paid the Federal Deposit Insurance Corporation, $27.3 million in settlements.

More than $11 million of the settlements came from individual bank directors and officers. The rest was from insurance companies, attorneys and a real estate firm.

The FDIC has authorized a total of 888 professional liability suits against those

THE ATLANTA JOURNAL-CONSTITUTION September 4, 2010
Failed banks pay $27.3M in settlements
they have determined played a role in a bank's failure. The agency has filed 54 such suits, including 15 in Georgia.

Bank	Date Failed	Settlement
American Southern Bank	April 24, 2009	$600,000
First Georgia Community Bank	Dec. 5, 2008	896,996
FirstBank Financial Services	Feb. 6, 2009	1,700,000
First National Bank	June 5, 2010	800,000
Georgia Bank	Sept. 25, 2009	10,100,000
Integrity Bank	Aug. 29, 2008	9,800,000
McIntosh Commercial Bank	March 26, 2010	85,000
Neighborhood Community Bank	June 26, 2009	1,800,000
NetBank	Sept. 28, 2007	100,000
RockBridge Commercial Bank	Dec. 18, 2009	700,000
The Community Bank	Nov. 21, 2008	740,000

The FDIC spared no one as State Senator Jack Murphy, who chaired the State Senate Banking Committee, was named in a lawsuit of the failed Alpharetta based Integrity Bank, where he was a Board member. Mr. Murphy was appointed in January 2011 to lead the Senate panel that oversaw state banking legislation. Mr. Murphy had also borrowed funds from The Bankers Bank to purchase his shares in Integrity Bank. FDIC eventually sued Mr. Murphy for non-payment of his stock loan.

It was commonplace for the FDIC to sue CEOs and Directors, where the failed bank had Directors & Officers Liability Insurance coverage. The FDIC assumed that if a bank failed the blame belonged to those overseeing and managing the bank, whether there was cause or not. In most cases the deep-pocket insurance companies chose to settle rather than defend their bank clients in court. In July 2014, the Georgia Supreme Court ruled that the FDIC would have to prove the Board's negligence, before it could expect to recover any damages from bank Officers, individual Directors, or their insurance companies.[93]

After my second daughter Gabrielle graduated from UGA, she began her working career at Aaron's Rents in Atlanta, a national company that specialized in leasing appliances, furniture, and electronics. Aaron's Inc.'s founder and chairman was Charles Loudermilk. Mr. Loudermilk, along with a group of well-to-do investors, chartered Buckhead Community Bank that subsequently failed in December 2009. On October 25, 2016, it was a defendant in one of the few unresolved failed bank lawsuits. And, one of the very few that would go all the way to trial and appeal. A civil jury returned a verdict of $4.98 million against several former directors and officers of the failed Buckhead Community Bank including Charles Loudermilk. The FDIC had been seeking $21.8 million. While the jury returned a verdict in favor of the FDIC on four of the loans cited in the suit, the jury found the defendants not liable for six other loans for which the FDIC sought recovery.[94]

The Court upheld the prior ruling that directors and officers were insulated from claims of negligence concerning the wisdom of their judgment. It did not, however, protect against "decision making that was made without deliberation, the requisite due diligence, or in bad faith". The verdict was appealed, and a final decision was pending. The outcome will serve as a "test case" for such future litigations.

Enterprise's failure along with most of the other victim banks can be attributed to bad economic conditions rather than fraud or fiduciary negligence. Without an insurance policy to lean on and no evidence of wrongdoing, it was unlikely that the FDIC would pursue a lawsuit against Management and the Board. Nevertheless, there was relief when the FDIC took no action during its three-year statutory limitation period. The deadline passed quietly in 2014.

On January 20, 2012, the Banking Department placed The First State Bank into receivership.[95] As cited in the AJC article, Hamilton State Bank with a FDIC "Loss Share" agreement in hand assumed control of the bank. At First State as was the case of Enterprise and other failed banks, the shareholders were left with worthless stock certificates...a sad scenario for what had been one of Georgia's most successful and profitable banks.

....

THE ATLANTA JOURNAL-CONSTITUTION January 24, 2012
Henry County bank seized
Branches to reopen today as Hamilton State Bank

By: J. Scott Trubey

The First State Bank, the last remaining bank based in Henry County, was seized and sold Friday by regulators. Hamilton State Bank based in Hoschton, acquired First State and its seven Henry branches in a loss-share transaction with the Federal Deposit Insurance Corp.

Henry has been among the hardest hit counties in Georgia's banking crisis. Ten banks that had at least a branch in Henry have failed, including the five that were based in the county when the Great Recession started.

Metro Atlanta's once surging Southside was once so hot community banks sprouted up or their headquarters there to tap into the real estate gold rush. But Stockbridge based First State was an old hand in Henry, founded in 1964. It also was the county's largest bank by deposits as of last June.

First State officials tried to hold through the real estate crisis. But the bank could no longer absorb losses from struggling borrowers, nor withstand plummeting real estate values, worsened in part by the local failures.

....

The First State Bank began in 1964 with a $200,000 capital investment from local citizens and grew to a $655 million bank with $70 million in capital before its demise. It was the quintessential community bank. Historically, its stock, Henry County Bancshares, Inc., was in great demand. The stock price had hovered around three times the bank's book value. Those who were fortunate to own shares were rewarded with ever-increasing quarterly dividends. David Gill, the son of a long-time community banker from Lavonia, became the CEO in 2001. His life time exposure to banking made him one of the more knowledgeable bankers in the area. As David stated in his final letter to the shareholders, "In its existence First State had paid out some $41 million in dividends." First State was the county's last remaining locally owned bank.[96] The failure of the ten banks operating in Henry County created a deep hole in the local economy.

....

THE ATLANTA JOURNAL-CONSTITUTION January 24, 2012
Henry left with no local banks

Real estate bust wiped out all five of county's hometown institutions.

Worry over loss of close working relationships

By: Tammy Joyner

A decade ago, few places rivaled Henry County for raw growth.

The Southside county was among the nation's fastest–growing, propelled by an unprecedented real estate boom. Feeding the gold rush: a cadre of home grown community banks that went on a land development and lending spree.

Now the county of about 204,000 people holds a new distinction. largest in Georgia county without a hometown bank.

All five of Henry locally owned banks failed during the shake out that followed the real estate bust.

It's just a sad, sad note out of this second Great Depression, "Henry Chamber of Commerce President Kay Pippin said. "The community banks have been a big part of the foundation that brought us to this point of growth." The First State Bank survived the longest because of a four decade relationship with customers. But even that wasn't enough to keep it from succumbing after it had joined the real estate rush.

Failed Henry County-based banks
The First State Bank, Stockbridge 1964 Jan 20, 2012
High Trust Bank, Stockbridge 1966 Jul 15, 2011
Enterprise Banking Company, McDonough 1925 Jan 21, 2011
FirstCity Bank, Stockbridge 1905 Mar 20, 2009
First Bank Financial Services, McDonough 2002 Feb 6, 2009

The closing of First State was as much a personal setback as was the plight of Enterprise...albeit in different ways. I had devoted thirty years of my working life to First State. To see the First State signs being taken down and replaced by Hamilton State was a heart breaker. Its 600 plus shareholders, 130 employees, and numerous customers would never again benefit from their hometown bank. The closing of the local banks did as much financial harm to Henry County as did the Boll weevil and General Sherman in years past. The recovery period would be long and slow.

For many years the Broders operated a dairy farm in Stockbridge. Completion of I-75 was a stimulus for area growth and changed the surrounding landscape from agricultural to residential. Dairy farming had become less feasible or practical resulting in the dairy farm transitioning into a beef operation. Like their neighbors who sold their land to developers, the Broders chose to develop some of their uncultivated farm land.

The Broder family venture also got caught up in the aftermath of local bank failures. St Margrit Village, named in memory of the mother and sister, was a development consisting a 54-lot subdivision catering to 55 and older residents. The development got off to a hot start in 2005, but like all other developments in Henry County, house and lot sales began to slow by the end of 2008. The $42,000 price tag for each lot comfortably covered the $27,000 development and $10,000 land costs. With little debt on the subdivision St Margrit Village was one of the few developments that escaped the numerous area bank foreclosures.

Photo taken on August 30, 2002 at University of Georgia's Animal and Dairy Science award and recognition dinner.

Standing left to right: Michael, Charles, Hans Jr., Hans Sr., Patrick, Peter and Josef Seated left to right: Margrit (Margie), Margrit and Angela

....

In Henry County the lending banks became the reluctant owners of foreclosed subdivisions and lots. The banks were strongly encouraged by regulators to sell non-performing and non-income producing real estate assets, even though there were few interested buyers. The stagnant housing market and developer defaults had added to the large inventory. The end result was the banks were selling lots at rock bottom prices.

United Community Bank had financed construction loans for the builders in St Margrit Village subdivision. The lone foreclosure was an un-improved lot that the builder had surrendered to the bank. In order to clean up its balance sheet United Community packaged its bank owned building lots and sold them to investors. The package included the St Margrit Village lot which it sold for $4,000.

Another situation involved a tract that adjoined the farm and was once owned by the Broders. The land ended up in the hands of an investor, who subsequently borrowed funds to develop the property. Separated from the farm to the east by I-75, Langley Oaks, a 77-lot high-density subdivision had original success, but was later surrendered to the bank by the developer. When the lending bank was closed by regulators, the loan was assumed by a "Loss Share" bank, that later foreclosed on the on the property and sold the lots for approximately $8,500 per lot.[95] The purchase price represented approximately 22% of the amount initially loaned to the developer by the failed bank.

The sale of the foreclosed developments and lots by the FDIC and/or "Loss Share" banks dramatically reduced lot values. It became evident to the Broders early on that selling lots at a breakeven price would prove difficult. The discounted sales had taken away the opportunity for the Broders to sell their lots for a realistic price. The saga of the St Margrit Village subdivision was testimony to how far reaching the housing meltdown was to property owners.

There were other unintended consequences of the bank failures. One such occurrence had an impact on a particular local charitable foundation. A former Director of First State, Bill Smith, established The William R. Smith and Sara Babb Smith Foundation. Mr. Smith was the owner of McDonough Equipment Company, who perfected and manufactured the Snapper Lawn Mower. Mr. Smith, a native Henry Countian, served as its president and chief executive from the late 1940s through 1979. Snapper for a time was one of the largest employers in Henry County with 1,100 employees.

It was Bill and Sara Smith's desire to leave a legacy that benefited the citizens of Henry County. In so doing, they established a Foundation, whose purpose and mission was to provide financial support for humanitarian, educational, and civic needs in Henry County. In addition to the initial cash contributed to the Foundation, the Smiths contributed a sizable amount of their Henry County Bancshares, Inc. (First State) shares. The stock dividends were used to fund the Foundation's various grant requests. The importance of the philanthropic contributions made to the deserving Henry County recipients cannot be over emphasized. Without the Henry County Bancshares, Inc. dividends, the Foundation's contributions were significantly reduced. Many grants would go under-funded or not funded at all.

CHAPTER EIGHTEEN

THE LAWSUIT

With the departure of First State, all of the banks, which I had counted on, were no longer there for me. Instead of the friendly bankers at McIntosh, RockBridge, Silverton, and First State, I now had to work with less sympathetic personnel at FDIC and Hamilton. It was now a challenge to restructure my outstanding debt that I had incurred in the purchase of Dorsey State Bank.

The reality of the closing of Enterprise Banking Company meant that my income was drastically reduced. The FDIC would most likely prevent any other commercial bank from offering me an executive position, thus ending my banking career. The probable closing of First State would then wipe out the largest portion of my remaining assets. Striving to be the largest shareholder in Enterprise seemed less important. I had religiously made reductions in the Dorsey State Bank acquisition loans, but I still owed a large sum.

As long as RockBridge and Silverton were in operation, all of the payments were made. However, after these banks were closed, my financial situation changed. I needed relief from the payments that were now dependent on my non-existent salary. FDIC, as Receiver for Silverton and RockBridge, was not interested in restructuring or modifying loans. Instead, it expected me to adhere to the original terms of the notes. To do so, I had to pay in full the upcoming balloon payment of the larger note and cope with the scheduled accelerated payments on the other. I had the misfortune of having to plead my case to the FDIC.

My loans that were well secured at the beginning were now backed by worthless stock. My first attempt to resolve the outstanding obligations was to encourage the FDIC to accept a discounted payoff. Since the FDIC had become an unsecured creditor, I assumed that it would be receptive to such a plan. The representative at FDIC RockBridge, Mr. Kamm, indicated that he would entertain an offer. Per his instructions I submitted a financial statement that detailed my declining financial position. I made every attempt to disclose all the information accurately.

Mr. Kamm and the FDIC took exception to certain transfers of real estate I had made during the term of the loan. Consequently, Mr. Kamm refused to consider any settlement and forwarded my file to the FDIC's Atlanta Regional Office. From then I was a marked man. If the FDIC had a "Most Wanted List", I would have been on it.

FDIC RockBridge became very aggressive in its collection effort of my loan. I was facing a difficult predicament… I could continue to pay, which I knew would not be for long, or jeopardize control over what little I had left. The consequences of my non-cooperative stance led to the FDIC filing suit in Fulton County on December 14, 2010. I was left with very few choices and needed help. I engaged Smith Welch Webb & White law firm from McDonough, Georgia, as legal counsel. I had known the attorneys in the firm for a long time and felt they would provide the best local representation available. It was the beginning of a lengthy legal battle.

It started with discoveries and depositions. Shawn Stafford from Neil, Robinson & Stafford representing FDIC RockBridge first deposed me. In return my attorney, Buddy Welch, deposed Ann Cross, who had originated the loan at RockBridge and the FDIC's contract Loan Officer, Andrew Kamm. Mr. Kamm had been assigned to handle my loan for FDIC RockBridge. Mr. Welch's questioning of Ms. Cross was courteous and brief, but less so for Mr. Kamm. Perry Mason would have been proud. Mr. Welch drilled Mr. Kamm for five hours. The pointed questioning did reveal facts that would have helped our cause. Mr. Welch completed his depositions by questioning a senior official from the FDIC Regional Office. It made for a long day.

It was our contention that RockBridge and the FDIC had failed to comply with their loan covenants, which required the bank's personnel to monitor the market value of the collateral. The loan covenant stated, if the stock value declined to less than 75% of the outstanding loan amount, the bank was required to sell stock to cover the short fall and bring the margin balance into compliance. Had the FDIC acted accordingly, shares of the Henry County Bancshares, Inc. stock could have been sold and the proceeds would have reduced the loan balance. As First State began to struggle, the marketing opportunity for the stock gradually disappeared.

At this time a monetary offer to settle the suit was made. The representatives at the bank level seemed receptive to an amount that was offered. I was told, however, that the settlement offer did not receive approval from the FDIC Atlanta Regional Office.

The State Court Judge Jay Roth considered the motions filed by both attorneys. But rather than issue a ruling, the Judge remanded the case to a Mediator for possible settlement. The Mediation hearing was held March 1, 2012, in the Charles L. Carnes Justice Center Building on Pryor Street in Atlanta. After the initial meeting of all the participants, the parties were divided into separate meeting rooms. The Mediator facilitated the negotiations by trying to encourage the two sides to find a happy medium between the offers and counter-offers that were presented. In the end the final settlement suggested by the FDIC was not workable. The 90-day cash payment was difficult, if not, impossible to meet. Without a settlement the FDIC went back to court to seek a summary judgment in its favor. The Judge declined its motion and the FDIC subsequently withdrew its lawsuit.

The quiet period did not last long as the FDIC filed a Civil Action in Federal Court on August 11, 2012. This lawsuit now included as defendants my wife Lyndy, my four children, and two Limited Liability Corporations in which I had an interest.[98]

The AJC made public the lawsuit in its business section expounding on the FDIC's allegations. The abbreviated newspaper article failed to mention that a substantial down payment had been made toward the purchase of the Dorsey State Bank. With the addition of the Henry County Bancshares, Inc, stock, the creditor banks had $2 worth of collateral for every $1 that they had loaned. I had invested a great deal of time and effort in attempting to resolve a difficult situation, not to mention, the significant amount I had paid in principal and interest. The article, however, would have the reader to believe that I had not acted in good faith and had every intention of defrauding the banks.

....

THE ATLANTA JOURNAL-CONSTITUTION August 14, 2012
Failed bank's CEO is sued

FDIC seeks payment from Enterprise exec, claims assets hidden.

By: J. Scott Trubey

A federal bank regulator issuing the former CEO of a failed Henry County bank, alleging he defaulted on loans and is sheltering assets in the name of relatives and various companies.

The Federal Deposit Insurance Corp. alleges Hans Broder, Jr., the former top officer of the failed Enterprise Banking Co. made property transfers to relatives and two companies "to hinder, delay, or defraud creditors" and is seeking repayment, according to two civil lawsuits filed this past week in U.S. District Court in Atlanta.

Broder allegedly defaulted on a nearly $912,000 loan issued in March 2005 by Silverton Bank, an Atlanta bank closed in 2009. He also is accused of defaulting on an $800,000 loan issued in April 2007 by RockBridge Commercial Bank, a Sandy Springs lender also closed in 2009.

Transferred ownership of eight properties, which the FDIC contends are worth more than $2 million "rendering Mr. Broder insolvent with insufficient assets" to pay

Failed bank's CEO is sued (cont.)

the debt both suits said.

Broder took out his Silverton loan using as collateral 5,000 shares of Enterprise stock.

He used as collateral more than 100,000 shares in the parent company of another Henry County lender, First State Bank, for the loan with RockBridge, the FDIC said.

I would now have to defend some earlier steps I had taken to protect my assets. The transfer of my half interest in our personal home and acreage to Lyndy occurred nearly two and half years before the Enterprise's closing. In refinancing the stock purchase loan at RockBridge, Lyndy had pledged her half interest in our Henry County Bancshares, Inc. stock as collateral. Since she did not receive any of the proceeds or financial benefit from the loan at the time, I had a tacit obligation to repay her for allowing me to risk her interest in the stock. I felt this transfer was justified.

I knew that if I were not able to work out a settlement with the FDIC, I would be facing a lawsuit, possible judgements and garnishments. With a judgement in hand the FDIC would be able to seize my bank accounts and obtain liens on all my personal properties as well as attach my interests in my other LLCs. Rather than to sit idly by, I chose to make some strategic transfers...some with the advice of legal Counsel. I knew the FDIC would question the strategy, but I determined that I would be in a better bargaining position if these assets were not solely in my name. It was a gamble. I admit I had not expected the FDIC to bring an action against not only me, but my family and business partner.

Although I had used a portion of retirement funds to purchase Dorsey State Bank, I still had a sizable sum. Since 401Ks and IRAs were immune from seizure, those funds and/or some of the transferred properties could be used to negotiate a settlement. I admit that I had a personal attachment to two properties conveyed to a family LLC. These I had purchased because they were at one time part of the farm. Two other rental properties I would have sold to apply toward the debt. However, the real estate market by then had depressed to a level that it was impossible to find a buyer much less receive a reasonable offer. At the time of the transfer the FDIC RockBridge and FDIC Silverton loans were either current or paid ahead. These transfers were made with the full intention of repaying the loans. All of the transfers occurred while I was gainfully employed, had the ability to pay, and prior to the closing of Enterprise. These transfers seemed to be defensible actions.

The twenty-two-page civil actions filed by FDIC RockBridge and FDIC Silverton accused us of having schemed to defraud the banks. The alleged value of the transfer in the petition was exaggerated. FDIC further alleged that the transfers occurred while I was insolvent…which, if proved to be true, could have possible criminal implications. The FDIC allegations were quite overwhelming to us, as no member of my family or circle of friends had ever been accused of such criminal behavior.

I was informed that the FDIC had an unwritten rule that a borrower was not allowed to transfer assets without authorization within a 5-year period after obtaining a loan. I had not been informed of such a requirement. The transfer information was disclosed on my financial statements submitted to the lending banks.

I was prepared to go toe to toe with the FDIC. The majority of the transfers were made when there was still an outside chance that Enterprise and First State would survive. The monetary values alleged by the FDIC lawyers had overstated the realistic value of the assets being transferred particularly the one-half interest in our home and one-third interest in land-locked farmland. The other disappointing aspect of the claim was that these two transfers occurred in 2008 well before my default. The Red Oak Road Investments, LLC stock transferred to Lyndy represented only a 50% interest in the company whose primary assets were commercial office warehouse buildings that carried sizable acquisition debt and had several unleased spaces at the time of the transfer. The cash that Lyndy received came from jointly filed tax return refunds. The proceeds were set aside as a reserve to pay the legal fees. Neither Lyndy nor I ever personally benefited from those funds. I estimated that the realistic value of the transfers was approximately one fourth of the amount the FDIC had alleged. I perceived the cleverly crafted FDIC complaint to be more fiction than substance. I reasoned that if the case could not be settled and eventually went to trial, any reasonable jury would side with us rather than the FDIC.

It was obvious that the FDIC's game plan was to use intimidation by involving as many parties as possible. Such a strategy resulted in my family members and friends being drug through the federal legal system. In its effort to prevail in its case against us, the FDIC engaged a high-profile legal firm named McGuire Woods who assigned the case to a group of lawyers headed by Robert Waddell. The fact that McGuire Woods was located off Peachtree Street on the 21st floor was an indication that the FDIC had hired a formidable and expensive law firm. Brian Strickland from a local law firm of Smith Welch was our attorney.

On May 1, 2013, my deposition took place at Smith Welch's office in McDonough. Present were Robert Waddell, Boyd Venable, and Barbara Rose representing the FDIC, and Brian Strickland representing us. The FDIC's attorney deposed me from 10:00 am to 5:00 pm with only a lunch break. Mr. Waddell did the questioning while Mr. Venable, the FDIC staff attorney, who traveled from the Jacksonville office, monitored. The questions ranged from the asset transfers to the review in detail of each financial statement submitted annually to the two banks from 2004 to 2011. It seemed that Mr. Waddell questioned every entry on each of the 8 annual financial reports. On May 2nd the depositions continued with Lyndy with some of the same questions. Hans III, Ashlee, and Gabrielle were next answering various questions as to the activities of the family company. Broder Enterprises III, LLC was the recipient of the some of the rental properties whose members included Lyndy, the four children and me.

Following the conclusion of the depositions and the sworn testimonies of the defendants, it was commonplace in civil cases for each side to consider a settlement. Mr. Venable, the in-house attorney for the FDIC, suggested a settlement that amounted to several hundred thousand dollars but less than I owed. I guess he felt some compassion for Lyndy and the kids. Mr. Waddell and Ms. Rose wanted no part of a settlement. They were duty bound to show no mercy to a CEO of a failed bank. The settlement amount was similar to the offer made by FDIC's counsel at the State Court mediation. I admit at that time I was still angry over the closing of Enterprise and not of the mindset to succumb to a cash offer, that I perceived to be unfair and excessive. I felt that I was a victim of circumstance not a perpetrator of a fraud.

I was disappointed in the FDIC's hard-line stance. It had been my strategy from the beginning to encourage the FDIC to come to the bargaining table. A path outside of the court system as a solution would be much easier and less costly. Unsuccessful, the litigation continued.

At the completion of the depositions, the FDIC requested additional financial information from all of the parties and later deposed Ronnie Hammond, my business partner and co-owner of the Red Oak Road Investments, LLC. I was informed on May 13th that the FDIC's attorney had served my tax preparer, Whaley, Hammonds, Tomasello, CPA, with a subpoena requesting copies all of my income tax returns dating back to 2004. It had already served my banks with subpoenas requesting our checking account records for that same period. The opposing law firm and the FDIC now had an enormous number of documents filled with information from which to build their case.

Brian deposed the FDIC's expert witness, Leanne Gould, an accountant. She was engaged by the opposing law firm to review the tax returns and financial information. FDIC had taken exception to my method of disclosing assets that were owned jointly with others. These assets were clearly identified on the financial statements, naming the co-owners and the percentage of ownership. I had always followed this format and none of the banks had ever objected. The banks seemed appreciative with the amount of detail that they were given. Ms. Gould had prepared a lengthy report that attempted to discredit my entries. What errors she uncovered would not have materially impacted my ability to pay the loans. Her conclusions and assumptions were argumentative. If admitted as evidence, would have helped our case.

With the conclusion of the depositions and information gathering process, both sides presented their summaries of their case's merits to Judge Thomas Thrash. I was disappointed, but not surprised, that Judge Thrash ruled on January 31, 2014, that I was responsible for the money that I owed RockBridge and Silverton. In so doing, the Judge granted the FDIC a partial judgment against me, but not against any of the other defendants. My family members and Ronnie were relieved. The Judge left the transfer of assets debate matter for a future jury to decide.

During the same period, my legal problems became more complex as a result of the collapse of the real estate market. In 2004 I participated in a residential development in the City of Jefferson, Jackson County. The area was growing with new industries moving into the area. Many of the new residents were commuting to Athens for employment. Mallard's Landing Planned Community was strategically located… a short distance from I-85 and near Jackson County High School. The public high school was considered as one of the best in the area. The 258-acre project, when completed, would yield approximately 400 lots. The land was to be purchased in stages. The project was to be developed in three phases over a period of time. I had been in several real estate ventures and had never lost money in any of them. The project was larger and more complicated than my previous ventures. However, the numbers looked good, and I was excited to be a partner.

Mallard's Landing was patterned after several other developments that my partners had successfully completed in the past. The project would have nice homes and an amenity package including a swimming pool and clubhouse. Since my partners each owned other properties in the area, they were available to oversee the project. The builders were lined up. First State agreed to do the financing for the borrowing entity, Westridge Partners III, LLC.

The first phase got off to a great start as the $200,000+ homes sold quickly. Since there was a lengthy lead time to complete of such projects, the partners obtained a second loan to begin the second phase and to purchase the remaining tract for the eventually third phase. The partners substantially increased their debt obligation unbeknown as to what lied ahead.

In early 2007, the builders began to experience a slowdown in home sales. The real estate market downturn occurred in Jackson County as it had in all of the other high growth areas. When the builders stopped buying the lots and Westridge Partners' cash began to dry up, the burden of making payments fell on the shoulders of the individual partners. The partners managed to keep the loans reasonably current through the end of 2011. Eventually, however, the company and the individual partners were no longer in a position to service the debt. First State was closed in January 2012 and Hamilton State Bank, as assignee, inherited the loans.

Since the partners had personally guaranteed the Westridge Partners III loans. Hamilton Bank's lawyers elected to sue the guarantors rather than foreclose on the real estate. As a consequence, Hamilton State was granted a judgment against me and the other investors on June 9, 2014.

CHAPTER NINETEEN

BANKRUPTCY

At the time Hamilton obtained the judgement on the delinquent loans it had as collateral numerous developed lots, a partially developed second phase and land available for a third phase. Although legal, it seems somewhat unfair to borrowers for creditors to sue before liquidating the collateral and incurring an actual loss.

Now I had two judgments against me and needed to take a more defensive and different course of action. I was advised by my attorney, Buddy Welch, to move the litigation from Federal Court to the U.S. Bankruptcy Court. Considering the relentless pursuit by the FDIC and Hamilton and the inability to reach a settlement, I elected to consult a bankruptcy attorney. My hopes were to get a fair hearing before a bankruptcy judge. The stigma of a bankruptcy was a personal embarrassment and further tarnished on my reputation. However, it was more important that these financial issues be resolved or discharged. I hoped of finding relief from the emotional stress that my family and I were enduring. We asked Brian Strickland to make a final settlement offer to the FDIC...which was rejected.

A Chapter 7 Bankruptcy is a legal proceeding that allows a debtor to seek debt forgiveness. In the olden days, debtors were generally imprisoned for not paying their bills. Once in prison they had no means to repay their creditors or obtain their freedom. With the prisons full, King George II of England shipped boat loads of debtors to his new Georgia colony. It is no wonder that the State of Georgia has the highest number of bankruptcy filings each year. It is an inherited trait.

Lyndy and I met with Gus Small of the Atlanta law firm of Cohen, Pollock, Merlin, & Small. Gus was a former bankruptcy Trustee and very knowledgeable of the inner workings of the bankruptcy court. Gus assured me that I had a better chance in bankruptcy court in getting an earlier hearing date and an eventual resolution, than I would in Federal Court. I filed a bankruptcy petition and had my first hearing on October 22, 2014.

In completing a bankruptcy petition, I was required to list all of my assets and liabilities and disclose my sources of income. These became a part of the bankruptcy estate and under the control of the Trustee. The Trustee was responsible for liquidating the assets and returning the net proceeds to the creditors. Fortunately, there were some exemptions. These included personal vehicles and household items that I was able to keep. My retirement accounts were fully exempt, and the various minority partnership interests received a reduced valuation. Since my bank stock holdings were worthless, I had few other assets to declare, other than the cash value in my whole life insurance policy. The amount of recorded judgments far exceeded the value of my assets. A sad outcome considering the real estate holdings and bank stocks were worth a considerable amount just a few years prior.

Gus and his staff handled the bankruptcy. The U.S. Bankruptcy Court Judge, Paul Bonapfel, appointed Barbara Stalzer as Trustee to oversee my bankruptcy estate. A petition to move the FDIC civil case from the Federal Court to the U.S. Bankruptcy Court was granted. Therefore, Mrs. Stalzer, who was an attorney, also assumed the legal duties on behalf of the FDIC in the fraudulent transfer case, as well as serving as bankruptcy Trustee. She assured all the parties that she was interested in settling the legal matter as soon as possible. I am not sure Mrs. Stalzer realized how complicated and time consuming her double duties would be. Regardless of the outcome, dealing with Mrs. Stalzer was less adversarial than dealing with the FDIC's attorneys.

I had only three creditors to satisfy...FDIC RockBridge, FDIC Silverton and FDIC "Loss Share" bank, Hamilton. In January 2015, the FDIC filed a complaint asking the court to declare my debts to be "non-dischargeable". The complaint alleged that because of the pending litigation I should not be given any relief from the FDIC's judgment. Ben Klehr, an associate of Gus Small, filed a 22-page rebuttal motion on February 10th. Judge Bonapfel later dismissed the FDIC's complaint.

In the meantime, our attorney, Lyndy, and I had our first meeting with Mrs. Stalzer on February 20th to begin discussions about the settlement parameters in regards to the alleged fraudulent transfers. McGuire Woods made all the case documents available to the Trustee. Stalzer engaged a CPA to analyze all my bank records. I spent the next two months providing Mrs. Stalzer with a sundry of documents and explanations. Mrs. Stalzer and her accountant were very thorough. During his review, the accountant discovered some recent income tax refunds that had been deposited into Lyndy's bank account rather than into our joint account. The Trustee filed a claim for the portion of the returns that had been paid by me. The majority of these funds had been used to pay legal expenses and were no longer available to the Trustee.

Gus was now having discussions with Walt Jones, who represented Hamilton, seeking his support for a settlement effort. Since Hamilton was now an unsecured creditor, in all probability, it would receive a larger share of the settlement proceeds through mediation than it could expect from a distribution of the bankruptcy assets. Rather than wait on the outcome of the litigation, Hamilton chose to support the mediation process, if the other parties agreed.

In May I received a call from Gus stating that the FDIC was ready to begin the mediation. I assume, it had gotten tired of paying all those attorney fees. It had finally realized that its share of the pie was shrinking by the day. As a condition of the mediation, Gus demanded a global settlement that included all creditors and the Trustee. Although there were several issues to resolve, the parties were able to reach an accord. June 30th was the date of the mediation meeting.

Mary Grace Diehl, a sitting U.S. Bankruptcy Judge, acted as Mediator. Ahead of the meeting, I had several thoughts as to what the outcome would mean if no settlement was achieved. Gus and Ben's prepared report for Judge Diehl detailed the possible scenarios that could result. In lawyer "speak" the abbreviated and paraphrased report described the complexity of my case and stressed the urgency to settle.

The report stated that if a global settlement was not possible, all sides will spend hundreds of thousands of dollars litigating this complex case. I will have to attempt to reach a unilateral settlement of the constructive fraudulent transfer claims with the Trustee. If that was successful, I will then contest the FDIC's ability to pursue claims outside of bankruptcy. If I win, then the FDIC's claims will be dismissed since they will have already been settled by the Trustee. If I lose, I will likely appeal. If the appeal was unsuccessful, the fraudulent transfer litigation will continue outside the bankruptcy case. I will then have to engage an expert witness and prepare for a trial on the intentional fraudulent transfer claims.

I will also continue to litigate the Non-dischargeability Action. If I win, then FDIC Silverton and FDIC RockBridge's unsecured claims will be subject to my bankruptcy discharge. If I lose, then the FDIC can try to collect on my non-exempt assets (which it knows are minimal and will be even more depleted after the settlement with the Trustee).

If no settlement is reached with the Trustee or the FDIC, then litigation continues on multiple fronts in the district court and the bankruptcy court. If the FDIC wins the Non-dischargeability Action, it will continue to pursue me for its judgments outside the bankruptcy case. If the FDIC and the Trustee win their fraudulent transfer cases against Lyndy and my children and void the transfers of property into their names, the FDIC and/or the Trustee would be left with property worth approximately half a million dollars and minority interests in various LLCs. We are left without our property, with huge non-dischargeable judgments against us, and without any liquid assets after spending hundreds of thousands of dollars for legal defense.[99]

Franklin Roosevelt called the bombing of Pearl Harbor "a day of infamy." To me the day of the mediation hearing was "a day of agony". One that would have a profound impact on the remainder of my life.

The meeting was held in the offices of McGuire Woods. I knew the place well since I had already been there for depositions. I remember the stiff $15 fee required to park in their garage. Lyndy and I met Ben and Gus there at 9:30 a.m. Each side was assigned a separate conference room to where Judge Diehl could privately deliver messages and settlement offers that were being exchanged between the opposing parties.

The day began with a meeting of all the participants in the main conference room. It was intimidating as each attendee, in turn, went around the table and make introductory remarks. It began with Judge Diehl at the head of the table being flanked by the Trustee, Mrs. Stalzer, and her accountant. Next was Mr. Waddell with two young assistant lawyers from McGuire Woods. The FDIC had three representatives including its legal counsel from Washington. Lyndy and I were represented by Gus Small and Ben Klehr. It was obvious from the onset that our side was outnumbered.

Judge Diehl made her appropriate opening remarks. The FDIC's spokesman was the next to speak. His remarks followed the pattern that the Board and I endured during the final meeting with the regulators following the examination. He enumerated all of the alleged wrongdoings that had led to the losses incurred by the FDIC. I spoke last and expressed my and my family's desire to reach a settlement. I told the group in a polite way that I could never forgive the FDIC for the harsh treatment that it and the other regulators had imposed on my Board and me during the final two years at Enterprise. I furthered stated that I resented the FDIC's contrary nature when I was trying to reach out for a settlement. I emphasized that a lot of money had been spent on attorneys by both parties which I considered unnecessary.

Each group then retired to its respective chambers. Judge Diehl suggested that we make the first offer. We had a predetermined amount that she could present to the Trustee and the FDIC. Judge Diehl returned, in what seemed to be two hours later, with a counter-offer that was totally unacceptable. It required cash that I did not have. At the encouragement of Gus, our offer was increased. As a compromise, the FDIC countered with a lesser cash figure and would accept the deeds to the rental properties. From Judge Diehl's feedback, it was apparent that there were too many negotiators in the opposing room having input. The negotiations drug on all day.

Gus stated, "That mediation could not be successful, unless both sides were unhappy with the final outcome." By now I had become quite aggravated and frustrated. Lyndy could not keep a dry eye. Finally, around 4:30 p.m. we came to a tentative agreement. Gus was correct. I was not happy with the outcome. I was disappointed in forfeiting most of my retirement funds, but I reconciled, it was only money and that the litigation would finally come to an end. All participants signed a handwritten Letter of Intent that included all the eventual terms and conditions.

On October 14, 2015, the agreement to settle was officially signed by all the parties and approved by Judge Bonapfel on November 24, 2015. In the ensuing months, I made my payment to the Trustee and transferred the properties as I had promised. The Trustee eventually sold the properties and distributed the proceeds to the creditors. In late 2016, Mrs. Stalzer abandoned the remaining assets of the bankruptcy estate, and Judge Bonapfel judicially discharged my remaining obligations to the FDIC and Hamilton. It was finally over!

CHAPTER TWENTY

EPILOGUE

My mother told me several times that I was a blessed child because I was born on a Sunday. My Uncle Albert, a parish Priest, was my God-father, and my Aunt Hilda, a nun, was my Godmother. My middle name was Melchior, my grandfather's first name. He was named after one of the three Wise Men as referenced in the Bible. My life with the help of divine guidance had been filled with success and happiness. I never foresaw Enterprise's failure or the misfortunes that followed. As I reflect back to all the events that transpired and given the opportunity to rewrite the script...I should have retired from banking earlier and moved to a chalet in the Swiss Alps.

Unbeknown at the time, Enterprise was probably doomed from the beginning. The rules of the game had changed. Hugh Morton referenced in his book to a "perfect storm". I contend, that the storm was already brewing. The launch of another bank in Henry County could not have come at a worse time. The banking environment that had been kind to investors had become unpredictable and laden with unanticipated risks. Enterprise's destiny was influenced by circumstances that could not have been foreseen or prevented. I wish that I had managed the bank differently and given a second thought to the types of loans that were being made. At the same time, if the Bank had received a little legislative or regulatory help, Enterprise may have survived. But now it is all in the past.

One has to wonder why the regulators were in such a hurry to close banks. The collateral damage to all the parties and overall costs were massive. Why did the regulatory agencies not place a moratorium on bank closings, except where there was apparent fraudulent activity? Instead, allow the economy to recover and then decide which banks deserved to be closed. The losses to the Depository Insurance Fund during the period would not be any greater. I remember the agriculture crisis in the 1980s. The Farmers Home Administration (FmHA) placed a two-year moratorium on farm foreclosures in 1983, while many banks slowed down their foreclosure efforts in spite of a record number of delinquencies.[100] The waiting period gave the government time to reevaluate the existing farm programs, meanwhile the banks took the opportunity to restructure the farmers' debts. Given the parallels, both the financial institutions and the farmers had serious financial problems in the 1980s. It was only the banks that experienced a repeat crisis in 2008. The regulators should have adopted the FmHA approach in dealing with the banking financial woes. Smart investors "buy low, sell high". FDIC's mindset was the total opposite, as it chose to liquidate bank assets at the bottom of the market.

The nation's large banks accounted for the majority of the bank deposits; however, community banks made 80% of the small business and agriculture loans. As to the future…I sadly predict that the smaller community banks in the larger metro markets face extinction. During 2019 the number of FDIC insured banks declined to 4,750 nationwide with only 200 community banks remaining in Georgia.[101] The community banks will be merged out by the larger financial institutions as competition and over-regulation make profitability for small banks difficult. Technology will replace the need for tellers, new account personnel, and loan officers. On-line banking and ATMs will now handle most of the customer banking needs. Willie Nelson's hit song about cowboys could easily apply to today's beleaguered bankers. "Don't let your babies grow up to be bankers!"

One has to question the merits of having Georgia community banks regulated by the Department of Banking and Finance, Comptroller of Currency, Federal Reserve, and FDIC all at the same time. With all those eyes looking over the shoulders of Georgia banks, how could so many of them fail? With the continuing onslaught of new regulations, there was too much effort spent in dealing with compliance and not enough time focusing on fundamental banking. Redundancy between the agencies that regulate banks created unnecessary costs for the banks. It was disappointing that the representatives in Washington continued to tinker with the banking system. The 1980 Saving and Loan and 2008 Banking Crises stemmed from poorly thought out legislation. The Dodd-Frank bill that followed was enacted to prevent such future crises. The "stress testing" of capital and the cumbersome reports required by all banks were intended to monitor the complicated large banks. Instead it was just another layer of regulations that created additional burdens on community banks. The reporting methods in existence prior to Dodd-Frank were adequate in measuring the community banks' financial health. Fortunately, Congress moved to roll back a portion of the 2,300-page Dodd-Frank Bill in May 2018.

Time has come to combine regulatory agencies and reduce the number of regulations. Small businesses including community banks are fed up with "out of control" government and Federal agencies that control all phases of their business operations. Whether, it is the FDIC, IRS, EPA, or the County code enforcer, there needs to be accountability. Do the ends justify the means? I do not believe that is the case today.

As a group the community banks were treated unfairly during this period. The closing of 10 banks in Henry County had created a local banking crisis. Had the regulators used more patience, most of the bank carnage could have been avoided. I remember a comment made by my friend David Gill, "The senior managers of the 90 something failed Georgia banks could not all be stupid." The same cannot be said about some of those who were entrusted to protect our banks. The losers were the communities and customers that the banks served. So were the shareholders and employees that had a vested interest in the banks. The winners were the "carpetbagger" investors who profited from resale of failed bank assets, as was the case in the purchase of Enterprise's main office building for a fraction of its value.

And then there was the tale of two banks. One bank benefited from the closing of two banks with offices in Henry County. Hamilton State Bank (Hamilton) was chartered in 2004 and was headquartered in Hoschton, a rural community in north Georgia. Like most start-up community banks, it grew quickly and was profitable in its early years. By 2006 the bank had reached $186 million in assets and earned $1.4 million. In 2008 Hamilton purchased Jefferson State Bank. It ended the year at $284 million in assets, but it suffered its first operating loss of $549 thousand. Like most of the area banks during that period, Hamilton incurred heavy losses of $2 million in 2009 and $2.2 million in 2010. As a troubled bank, it shrank its balance sheet and reduced staff in order to preserve capital. In its quests to replenish its shrinking capital position, it found an investor group. The out of town investors injected capital and provided the necessary funding to participate in the FDIC's Loss Share programs. Hamilton also received $7 million in TARP funds.[102]

In 2011 Hamilton was the successful bidder for the acquisition of two failed banks, Bartow County Bank in Cartersville and McIntosh State Bank in Jackson. At the end of 2011, Hamilton grew to a $909 million bank with 220 employees and earned $6.8 million. In 2012 Hamilton acquired The First State Bank of Stockbridge. At the end of 2012, Hamilton reached $1.38 billion in assets and earned $16.5 million. In 2013 Hamilton acquired the failed Douglas County Bank in Douglasville. Now Hamilton was under 4 five-year "Loss Share" programs, whereby the FDIC was reimbursing Hamilton 80% of the losses incurred from most of its acquired loans. Hamilton earned $8.6 million in 2013. By the end of 2015, Hamilton State Bank was a $1.7 billion bank with 358 employees. It earned $15.4 million and was the 481st largest bank in the U.S.[103] Hamilton State merged with Ameris Bancorp of Moultrie in 2018.

The other bank, Enterprise, with a similar beginning had a different ending. Neglected, forsaken, and alone it could not survive in its unfamiliar banking environment. As Charles Dickens wrote; "It was the best of times, it was the worst of times, it was the spring of hope, and it was the winter of despair." Enterprise was closed on January 21, 2011, a cold and gloomy day.

Those in the know should have seen a banking crisis coming. The nation was experiencing a robust economy with full employment, yet foreclosures were on the rise…an unprecedented occurrence in U.S. history. This early warning sign should have alerted the leaders that something was amiss. Washington's goal to make every American family a homeowner was an unrealistic Utopian dream. Introducing "Mark to Market" accounting rules during a recession was a recipe for disaster. The wholesale closing of banks was the wrong approach in resolving the nation's economic woes.

The FDIC was overly aggressive with its Consent Order in prohibiting Enterprise from renewing its Brokered Deposits. The mandate needlessly threatened its liquidity and could have prematurely closed the Bank. A cap on total amount of Brokered Deposits and a timetable to replace those deposits with local deposits would have been a more practical approach.

Enterprise's capital ratio fell below the 2% threshold as a result of the write down of two loans. The examiners considered the underlying collateral of a $2,000,000 loan worthless. The City of McDonough's Impact Fee Credits were valued in excess of $3,000,000 and could have been sold to anyone needing to pay for an impact fee. All new construction in the City of McDonough required the upfront payment of an Impact Fee which the City used for anticipated future infrastructure expenses. Those seeking a building permit could most likely purchase a credit at a discount from the borrower or holder of the credits, instead of paying the full price to the City. The questionable collateral had value. The Bank should have been allowed to recognize that value on its books, not be required to write all of the amount down.

The second loan was a loan secured by undeveloped commercial property on Highway 95 in Fayetteville. The property value had declined and was worth less than the loan amount. The examiners had determined a write down of $700,000 was necessary to cover the eventual loss, if and when the property was sold. The loan had four guarantors. One of which had a sizable net worth and the means to ensure the Bank it would not incur a loss. The single-pay loan was delinquent at the time of the examination but was renewed after the examination. With the existing ability to pay the loan Management should have been given the opportunity to restructure the loan to bring it into compliance, not written down.

My adversarial relationship left me with much scorn and contempt toward the Georgia Department of Banking and FDIC. They had become powerful bureaucracies whose actions deserved public scrutiny. When the FDIC announced the closing of Enterprise in January 2011, it estimated that the Bank's failure would cost the Deposit Insurance Fund $39.6 million. It was hard to image that the administrative cost, the market value of the bank buildings, and value of the $72 million in loans still on the books would account for such a large loss. Enterprise had its share of troubled loans that were secured by diminished valued real estate, but it also had just as many performing loans.

One has to wonder about the FDIC's cost management in liquidating failed banks and question the administrative costs, the discounts offered to failed bank borrowers, the amount investors were allowed to bid at auctions, and the prices accepted for its inherited bank assets. Was the FDIC efficient in managing costs, while obtaining a reasonable return for the assets it assumed from Enterprise? Too many assets were sold for a fraction of their real value. Those that had invested in Enterprise were the ultimate losers. Those that owned real estate in the area saw their property values plummet. The tragedy was the misery that the citizens endured while watching others profit from their misfortunes. The transfers of wealth that occurred during this period left the ill-fated individuals with little hope of recovering their losses.

My legal problems were traumatic and resulted in a long drawn out and expensive ordeal. I knew the responsibilities and risks in borrowing money and the probable consequences, if not repaid. It took a sitting bankruptcy judge to resolve the disputes in mediation. It was par for the course that the FDIC needed four attorneys to hammer out its conditions for a settlement. As the regulator and as the eventual creditor, the FDIC was too inflexible and unreasonable in some of its demands and expectations. The regulators contributed to my financial problems. They closed Enterprise which eliminated the source of my income. They closed Silverton and RockBridge which removed any possible restructure of my loans. They closed First State Bank, whose stock served as collateral for the loans. Yet, the FDIC aggressively pursued me in court before finally settling.

As a part of my settlement, I turned over to the Trustee a majority of my retirement accounts, a portion of the cash surrender value of a life insurance policy, a duplex, and a commercial building. Considering the amount, I had paid in interest and principal on the loans to RockBridge and Silverton, the legal fees I paid in attempting to settle, and the value of the real estate and cash paid to the Trustee, the total I expended was not far from the unpaid principal balance of the loans in question. However, after deducting the legal fees FDIC had paid its attorneys and the cost for all the time and energy expended by the its personnel, the net amount the FDIC received was less than what it could have received four years earlier. In reality the losers were the Depository Insurance Fund and the banks that contributed to the Fund through their assessments.

As for Hamilton, it incurred only minimal, if no losses at all, from the Westridge Partner's loans. The FDIC reimbursement as part of the "Loss Share" agreement and the proceeds from the sale of the real estate collateral probably covered Hamilton's shortfall.

I remember Glenn's prophetic remark after I had informed him in a conciliatory fashion of Enterprise's certain fate. He said to me, "**This too shall pass**." I believe that he had correctly predicted the outcome. Unfortunately, Glenn died in September 2014 from cancer and was not here to help write the final chapter.

As for the staff in Abbeville, all found employment at other local banks. Jill McDuffie, Operations Officers, moved to Wilcox State Bank. As the only remaining bank in Abbeville and with Jill's help, Wilcox State Bank flourished with its newly inherited customers from Enterprise. Not all of the McDonough staff, who were employed at Enterprise Banking Company during its existence and at the time of closing, resumed their banking careers. Many were emotionally scarred from the experience and no longer envisioned a bright employment future at the local banks. Banking positions were now a scarcity. Most, however, did land on their feet. Julie Coile finished her undergraduate degree and found a position at Clayton State University. Jessica Richards, Operations Officer, returned to her former bank, which had been acquired by United Community Bank. Rhonda Foster, Mortgage Officer, returned to her former bank, which became Hamilton State Bank. Leslie Waits found employment at First Fidelity, which had acquired the closed First Henry Financial Services' building. Tanya Lasseter, Head of Bookkeeping Operations, returned to school to pursue her college degree and later found employment at State Bank in Macon. All gained valuable experience by working for a small community bank. The lessons learned at Enterprise gave them awareness and knowledge of banking that they could not have gleaned from a text book.

- As to some of the others mentioned…sadly Mr. Henderson also passed away in 2014.
- As of 2017 and at age of 68, Hugh Morton was diagnosed as cancer free and climbed the Casablanca and Villa Rica Mountains in Patagonia, Argentina.
- Bob Prather left Gray Communications and now owns several TV stations.
- Mark Conner, Audrey Price, and Pamela Moss remain in prison.
- Judy Coker has retired from banking and has become a Master Gardner.
- Shailendra settled his lawsuit with his aggrieved investors.
- Mark Brittain lives in Stockbridge and now has his own firm. Mark is a general practice lawyer and enjoys representing clients from the grass roots of the community.
- David Gill heads the Henry County Chamber of Commerce.
- Heather Bledsoe mentioned in the NPR story is in the flower and wedding business. She operates out of her home and never purchased the property in Locust Grove that the banks would not finance.
- Buddy Welch, my attorney, was killed in 2018 when struck by a train.

I wish the story had a better ending. George Bailey in "It's A Wonderful Life" had the generous citizens of Bedford Pines raise the money to save his bank. As for me, my life's work as a banker was tarnished by the sad ending of Enterprise. The outcome, however, cannot take away the memories of the special relationships that I was able to develop during the 35 years as a community banker. I take pride in the number of people that I was able to help through lending and providing financial advice. I made thousands of consumer and personal loans. There were numerous small business loans. Some were unsuccessful, but the majority endured and provided a livelihood for its owners and its employees.

I will mention one commercial loan that led to a successful grocery chain. Gerald Taylor and Raymond Johnson, who were former employees of Food Giant, desired to purchase Stockbridge's lone grocery store. The store and its owner had encountered financial difficulties. Gerald and Raymond were able to acquire the store and turn the business around. At last count their company operated 55 Quality Food grocery stores.

I was a believer that viable communities needed churches. I had encouraged the loan officers to make loans to those of all faiths. The bank never incurred any losses from these endeavors. I felt I did my part in the building of the community. As I travel throughout the county, I see a landscape dotted with homes, commercial buildings, and small businesses that benefited from loans that I had a hand in originating.

Our goal of creating a successful banking operation did not materialize, but many benefited in a positive way from the effort. Ending on a quote from an anonymous author "I started out with nothing, and I am happy to report I still have most of it." There is much more to life than just money. Good health with a supportive family is the real treasure.

ABOUT THE AUTHOR

Hans Melchior Broder, Jr. was born on July 6, 1947 in Bern, Switzerland and immigrated with his parents to Stockbridge, Georgia, in 1951. He was raised on the family's dairy farm, where he presently lives, and is the oldest of eight children. He is married and has four children and ten grandchildren. He received a bachelor's degree in Business Administration from University of Georgia and began his working career as a Business Education teacher at Stockbridge High School in 1969. In 1971 he accepted a lending position with The First State Bank and remained with the Bank until his retirement in 2001. He was the Organizer and CEO of Enterprise Banking Company until 2011.

ENDNOTES

1. Deposit Market Share Wilcox County, FDIC Summary of Deposits as of June 30, 2006, Federal Deposit Insurance Corporation, official website, https://www.fdic.com

2. Dorsey State Bank Financial Statements prepared by Donnie Luker, CPA, Mauldin-Jenkins

3. Jeylin White, "Henry Businessman A Pillar of the Community", *Henry Herald*, January 30, 2013

4. Henry Unger, "The key to life is persistence", *Atlanta Journal-Constitution*, March 3, 2013

5. Georgia Department of Banking and Finance, official website, https://georgia.gov/organization/department-banking-and-finance

6. Federal Deposit Insurance Corporation, official website, https://www.fdic.com

7. Federal Reserve Bank, official website, https://federalreserve.gov

8. U.S. Bureau of Labor Statistics, Bank Examiners, https://www.usa.gov

9. Myers – Briggs, Type Indicator adapted for Psychological Types by Carl Jung, 1923

10. Ralph Nader, *Unsafe At Any Speed*, 1965

11. 5 Cs of Credit, *Investopedia*, https://www.investopedia.com

12. Appraisal Methods-Mortgage101, https://www.homes.com

13. Enterprise Shareholder List from shareholder records of Enterprise Banking Company, Inc.

14. Georgia Department of Banking and Finance, official website, https://georgia.gov/organization/department-banking-and-finance

15. Bureau of Labor Statistics, Unemployment Rate in Henry County, Ga., https://www.usa.gov

16. Greg Hambrick, "Bankruptcy Rates in Georgia: Where are People Struggling the Most?", August 10, 2016

17. Investopedia Staff, Case Study: "The Collapse of Lehman Brothers", Updated February 16, 2017

18. Kimberly Amadeo, "Stock Market Crash of 2008", *U.S. Economy*, April 3, 2017

19. Adam Hayes, CFA "Economic Basics: Supply and Demand", *Investopedia*, November 7, 2021, https://www.investopedia.com

20. Staff, "Troubled Banks", *Atlanta Journal-Constitution*, March 2013

21. 2007 Enterprise Financial Statement from annual reports prepared by Cliff Williams, CPA, Mauldin-Jenkins

22. Oonaugh McDonald, "Repeal of the Glass-Steagall Act: Myth and Reality", *CATO Institute*, November 16, 2016, https://www.cato.org

23. "Big Ga. Banks Win Branching Battle", *American Banker*, July 1998, https://www.americanbanker.com

24. Jeffry Pilcher, "Why Are Credit Unions Tax Exempt? Do You Really Know?" *The Finance Brand*, December 21, 2010, https://thefinancebrand.com

25. Georgia Department of Banking and Finance, official website, https://georgia.gov/organization/department-banking-and-finance

26. Wikipedia, Credit Unions in the U.S., https://en.wikipedia.org

27. Clark Howard, "Switching To A Credit Union Can Be Best Move", December 6, 2012

28. American Bankers Association, "Credit Unions Tax Exemption Adds To Federal Debt, Spring 2016

29. Kimberly Amadeo, "How Interest on the National Debt Affects You", *U.S. Economy*, July 6, 2016

30. Wikipedia, Market-to-Market Accounting, https://en.wikipedia.org

31. Wikipedia, FDIC Deposit Insurance Corporation, https://en.wikipedia.org

32. Wikipedia, Government National Mortgage Association, https://en.wikipedia.org

33. Wikipedia, Housing and Community Development Act 1992, https://en.wikipedia.org

34. Wikipedia, Taylor, Bean & Whitaker, https://en.wikipedia.org

35. Holden Lewis, "The basics of private mortgage insurance, or PMI", *Bank Rate*, March 28, 2018, https://www.bankrate.com

36 Federal Deposit Insurance Corporation, official website, https://www.fdic.com

37. Hugh Morton, *The Great American Housing Fiasco*, 2011

38. Wikipedia, Troubled Asset Relief Program, https://en.wikipedia.org

39. Wikipedia, Wachovia Is Now Wells Fargo, https://en.wikipedia.org

40. Russell Grantham, "Silverton's Rise and Fall", *Atlanta Journal-Constitution*, August 28, 2011

41. Wikipedia, Bankers Banks, https://en.wikipedia.org

42. Russell Grantham, "Silverton's Rise and Fall", *Atlanta Journal-Constitution*, August 28, 2011

43. Southern Community Bank, Fayetteville, Ga., Federal Deposit Insurance Corporation, official website, https://www.fdic.com

44. Neighborhood Community Bank, Newnan, Ga., Federal Deposit Insurance Corporation, official website, https://www.fdic.com

45. Peralte C. Paul, "RockBridge Commercial Bank Closed By Regulators", *Atlanta Journal-Constitution*, December 18, 2009

46. CAMALS ratings, Federal Deposit Insurance Corporation, official website, https://www.fdic.com

47. Loan Classifications, Federal Deposit Insurance Corporation, official website, https://www.fdic.com

48. Stephen Simpson, "Texas Ratio Rounds Up Bank Failures", *Forbes*, October 28, 2008

49. John Maxfield, "Why Almost Every Bank in Texas Failed in 1980", *Motley Fool*, April 22, 2015

50. J. Scott Trubey, "House Passes Bill to Study Rescue Efforts", *Atlanta Journal-Constitution*, July 30, 2011

51. J. Scott Trubey, "Regulators called too tough" *Atlanta Journal-Constitution*, August 17, 2011

52. 2009 Enterprise Financial Statement from annual reports prepared by Cliff Williams, CPA Mauldin-Jenkins

53. "Georgia Banks still hurting", *Atlanta Journal-Constitution*, FIG Partners, August 17, 2017

54. Peter Carbonara, "Banking: Mr. Cleanup", *Business Week*, October 29, 2009

55. Russell Grantham "Builder's fall just one link in chain", *Atlanta Journal-Constitution*, March 15, 2009

56. Kathy Lohr, "When Georgia Banks Fail, Small Businesses Suffer", NPR August 15, 2009

57. Purchase and Assumption Agreement, Federal Deposit Insurance Corporation, official website, https://www.fdic.com

58. Paul Donsky, "Banks under the gun to raise more cash", *Atlanta Journal-Constitution*, November 16, 2009

59. Joe Rauch, "Feds seize First Georgia Community Bank", *Atlanta Business Chronicle*, December 5, 2008

60. McIntosh State Bank, *Citybizlist*, October 27, 2009, https://boston.citybizlist.com

61. Loss Share Agreements, Federal Deposit Insurance Corporation, official website, https://www.fdic.com

62. Insured Deposits, Federal Deposit Insurance Corporation, official website, https://www.fdic.com

63. Johnny Jackson, "FDIC-insured McDonough bank fails", *Henry Daily Herald*, January 25, 2011

64. J. Scott Trubey, "Closing failed banks emotional experience", *Atlanta Journal-Constitution*, March 15, 2010

65. Henry County Georgia Property Tax Records, official website, https://www.henrycountytax.com

66. Shaila Dewan, "A Small Town Loses A Pillar", "Its only bank". *New York Times*, March 27, 2009

67. Shareholder Letter, Enterprise Banking Company, Inc., January 22, 2011

68. Deposit Market Share Henry County, FDIC Summary of Deposits as June 30, 2006, https://www.fdic.com

69. List of Enterprise Banking Largest Loan Loss Customers, Enterprise Banking Company, Inc. shareholder records

70. John Engen, "When The Devil Went Down To Georgia", *Bank Director. Com*, July 20, 2012

71. Kimberly Amadeo, "Tarp Bailout Program...Did Tarp Help You or the Bank", *U.S. Economy*, April 4, 2017

72. Georgia Department of Banking and Finance, official website, https://georgia.gov/organization/department-banking-and-finance

73. Alan Judd, "Who is Watching the Banks ", *Atlanta Journal-Constitution*, June 19, 2011

74. Federal Deposit Insurance Corporation Improvement Act of 1991, Federal Deposit Insurance Corporation, official website, https://www.fdic.com

75. Richard R. Cheatham, "Open Letter to GBA", November 17, 2011

76. Mark Sunshine, "Kill It Before It Eats Us Alive", *Seeking Alpha*, September 29, 2008

77. List of Failed Banks in Georgia, Bankrate.com from 2007 to 2016, https://www.bankrate.com

78. Jason Smith, "Henry bankruptcies second highest in nation", *Henry Daily Herald*, January 26, 2011

79. Georgia Bureau of Investigation, Crime Statistic Summary Report of Henry County 2005-2015, https://www.gbi.georgia.gov

80. Smart Numbers, *Atlanta Journal-Constitution*, June 12, 2012

81. Misty Williams, "Sales rise slightly for existing homes", *Atlanta Journal-Constitution*, January 16, 2012

82. Noelle Nipour, "Loss Share Abuse Public" *SunSentintal*, April 14. 2013

83. Rick Woods, "FDIC Loss-Share Agreement Scam Killing America". February 4, 2012

84. J. Scott Trubey & Tammy Joyner, "Move to Henry proves costly", *Atlanta Journal-Constitution*, March 15, 2009

85. Jon Prior, "Georgia Banker gets 12-year Sentence for Fraud", *Housewire*, August 8, 2012

86. J. Scott Trubey, "Charges added against ex-banker", *Atlanta Journal-Constitution*, April 24, 2014

87. J. Scott Trubey & Bill Torpy, "Land deals crumble into cries of fraud", *Atlanta Journal-Constitution*, January 28, 2011

88. J. Scott Trubey & Bill Torpy, "Feud heats up in land dealings", *Atlanta Journal-Constitution*, January 28, 2011

89. J. Scott Trubey "Fed sue law firm and in bank collapse", *Atlanta Journal-Constitution*, February 9, 2011

90. Russell Grantham, "Silverton's Rise and Fall", *Atlanta Journal-Constitution*, August 28, 2011

91. Juan Ignacio Blanco, "Pamela Carole Moss", *Murderpedia*, June 2012, https://murderpedia.org

92. Arielle Kass, "Failed banks pay $27.3M in settlements", *Atlanta Journal-Constitution*, September 4, 2010

93. Kevin LaCroix, Failed Bank Litigation: Jury Returns $5 Million Verdict Against Failed Bank's Former Directors", *The D&O Diary*, October 25, 2015, https://www.dandodiary.com

94. Kevin LaCroix, "Georgia Supreme Court Affirms, Elucidates Business Judgment Rule – Its Limitations", *The D&O Diary*, July 14, 2014 https://www.dandodiary.com

95. J. Scott Trubey, "Henry County bank seized", *Atlanta Journal-Constitution*, January 24, 2012

96. Tammy Joyner, "Henry left with no banks", *Atlanta Journal-Constitution*, January 26, 2012

97. Henry County Georgia Property Tax Records, official website, https://www.henrycountytax.com

98. J. Scott Trubey, "Failed bank's CEO is sued", *Atlanta Journal-Constitution*, August 14, 2012

99. Gus S. Small, "Letter to Judge Mary Grace Diehl," May 20, 2015

100. Jason Manning, "The Midwest Farm Crisis of the 1980s", *The Eighties Club*

101. Federal Deposit Insurance Corporation, official website, https://www.fdic.com

102. Carolyn Crist, "Hamilton State Bank Sells Stock", *Gainesville Times*, March 5, 2011

103. Uniform Bank Performance Report, "Hamilton State Bank", Federal Deposit Insurance Corporation, official website, https://www.fdic.com

INDEX OF NAMES

Made in United States
Orlando, FL
27 August 2022

21633966R00134